Praying with Mom

Praying with Mom

The Journey of Tears, Love, and Spiritual Growth

MICHAEL CHUNG

RESOURCE *Publications* • Eugene, Oregon

PRAYING WITH MOM
The Journey of Tears, Love, and Spiritual Growth

Copyright © 2012 Michael Chung. All rights reserved. Except for brief quotations in critical publications or reviews, no part of this book may be reproduced in any manner without prior written permission from the publisher. Write: Permissions, Wipf and Stock Publishers, 199 W. 8th Ave., Suite 3, Eugene, OR 97401.

Resource Publications
An Imprint of Wipf and Stock Publishers
199 W. 8th Ave., Suite 3
Eugene, OR 97401
www.wipfandstock.com

ISBN 13: 978-1-61097-909-2
Manufactured in the U.S.A.

All scripture quotations, unless otherwise indicated, are taken from the Holy Bible, New International Version®, NIV®. Copyright ©1973, 1978, 1984 by Biblica, Inc.™ Used by permission of Zondervan. All rights reserved worldwide.

This book is dedicated to all the brothers and sisters in Christ around the world who prayed for my mother. There is no doubt, her life would have been very different had you not prayed for her.

2 Corinthians 1:11 "as you help us by your prayers. Then many will give thanks on our behalf for the gracious favor granted us in answer to the prayers of many."

Contents

Acknowledgments ix
Foreword by Robert Coleman xi

1 Journey of the Heart 1
2 Unbelief 8
3 Pain 14
4 Providence 21
5 Prayer 30
6 Refreshment and Hope 36
7 Darkness and Forgiveness 42
8 Prayer, a Second Look 52
9 Pride 56
10 Insecurity 63
11 Finding Love 70
12 When the Unexpected Changes Your Life 78
13 Unpredicted Friends 84
14 Romance and Respite 91
15 Wedding Day 103
16 Preparing to Say Goodbye 107
17 Grief 114
18 Why? 118
19 See You in Heaven 122

Foreword

ONE OF THE MAIN priorities of our lives is to disciple men and women. Mentors must disciple their mentees by living life together. The real laboratory of the world is the best place for discipleship to happen.

Discipleship requires example. Example gives credibility. People are far more impressed by what they see than what they hear.

The path to discipleship involves experiencing life's ups and downs. It is easy for believers to be Disciples of Christ when life is going well but the real test of true faith involves belief and obedience when times are difficult. When walking through the Valley of the Shadow of Death, does one leave their faith, being angry at God for allowing them to experience trials and hardships or does one draw closer to our Lord, trusting that experiencing the fellowship of suffering is just as important as experiencing Christ's resurrection power.

In this book, Dr. Michael Chung gives us a glimpse into dealing with life's losses and an inside look into his heart. When suffering occurs, how do we deal with it? How do we allow it to draw us closer to Christ? How do we make sense of things when life comes crashing down? These are the types of issues that are dealt with in this book. It is a rare glimpse into one's life when dealing with one of the most difficult tragedies: when a loved one suffers. From the first day of hearing the news to the last day of saying goodbye and everything in between, Michael Chung shares with us his life of ups and downs and how he believes God used it to draw him closer to Himself. This gives us an example to follow in times of difficulty and disappointment when it seems God is silent, but in reality, He is closer than ever before.

Robert Coleman
Wilmore, KY

Acknowledgments

First, I want to thank Christian Amondson and those at Wipf and Stock Publishers for allowing me the opportunity to share the world my story and journey.

Vicki Chiu has not only been a great friend to my wife and I but also a great help in the writing process. Thank you for taking time to read through my manuscript and offer thorough and honest comments. Your life is an example to all and I am so glad to have your eyes and your heart in this project.

Lana Witt spend hours proofreading, editing, and reading all my manuscripts despite a busy schedule, living in a foreign country and mothering her first child, beautiful Anabel. I am so grateful that you took your time to help and appreciate how you modeled an attitude of godliness and service. You viewed your work as ministry and felt that if this book could help just one person, it was worth the hours of time you put in.

As if a dedication page is not enough, to all those who labored with me in prayer and support during the time of my mother's battle, I again thank you. Many of you replied to my emails and encouraged me to write these thoughts in book form. Since you were so gracious to pray and love, I have obliged and done the best I could to express my thoughts in book form.

Jodi, my wife, was not a part of my life when the journey first began but was indispensible during the later part. Your mother-in-law always wanted a daughter and the last few months of her life, she got one. You are proof that there is a God (no way I could have gotten you if there wasn't) and that when we trust God with all our life, He will move when time is best.

Finally, I thank my mom for loving me all of my life and teaching me that time with loved ones is our most valuable asset. Though you are in heaven now, you are in my heart forever and I cannot wait to get to the gates of heaven and see you there.

1

Journey of the Heart

In his heart a man plans his course, but the LORD determines his steps.

—PROVERBS 16:9

My dear brother, let God make of you what he will,
he will end all with consolation,
and shall make glory out of your suffering.

—SAMUEL RUTHERFORD

LIFE IS LOSS. ALL humanity desires to avoid it, but loss is unavoidable, making life difficult. Loss takes many forms: a natural disaster strikes bringing sudden and unexpected devastation. Someone we love and prepare to commit our life to abruptly ends the relationship. A healthy person becomes sick. A spouse commits adultery and wants a new life with someone else. A father passes away before giving his daughter away in marriage. A job is lost. Thieves rob a home. A rapist attacks. A business loses profitability overnight. A church splits. A leader quits. Terminal disease strikes a family member. The list goes on and on and on.

The hardest loss to experience is the loss of love. Most people want a life with little hardship and no loss, where love and loved ones live forever. Loss makes life difficult for all of us, because at some point everyone greets it face to face.

Difficulty visited my home with the shocking news of my mother's stage 4 lung cancer diagnosis. She was always healthy, so rarely sick, and her parents lived into their upper 90's. Mom appeared to have their genes. However, life has a way of changing without our notice, and the unexpected becomes the expected.

I believe mothers make the world go 'round. Without them nothing can happen, and humanity is lost. They not only give life, but also nurture it.

Not everyone has a good relationship with their mother. Some people have cruel moms who treat them horribly; others have distant moms, unloving and extraordinarily selfish. Some moms physically abandon their children; others emotionally abandon them. Many people cry out because of wounds inflicted in their soul by a mother.

Some women deeply desire to be a mother and carry the burden of being unable or temporarily prevented. Others desire motherhood only to find it less than fulfilling once it arrives. Pain can obviously and easily be associated with motherhood.

MOTHER'S INNER STRENGTH

Mine is a different story. My mother and I were very close. From the age of nine years old and on, she was the only parent for my brother and I. Dad tragically and suddenly died on a business trip while swimming close to the La Jolla beach area in San Diego. He drowned in a rip current. Mom was left with no job and two young children she needed to raise. This was not the life she signed up for, but the loss of my dad didn't stop her from being a dedicated mom to fatherless sons. She easily could've disassociated from life or even disassociated from her children, but she drew from an inner strength and maternal instinct that allowed her to have enough fortitude to carry on.

Never did I sense resentment from her, nor did I feel that she felt her life was held back. If she did, she never mentioned it. Mom focused on making sure her two sons grew up in as normal of an environment as they could. We always had clothes to wear, shoes to walk in and food on the table. We were able to receive new bikes for birthdays, gifts under Christmas trees, and vacations in the summer. Though we'd lost our father at an early age, mom made an effort to raise us without feeling we were less than children that had their father. She did a great job!

Journey of the Heart

Who is my mom? She could be described as a real character. Many Asians are quiet and reserved, often finding it difficult to express feelings. Not my mother. She was honest, direct, and very winsome. People quite naturally and quickly loved her. A gregarious personality, she often chided people with a smile while being a gifted peacemaker. It was common for women to come to our house late at night after a fight with their husband seeking my mother for wise counsel and a comforting spirit. I remember many nights hearing her friend's tears, then mother's voice exhorting them not to give up and to carry on. She was often invited to visit homes after a dispute to help make peace between two parties stubbornly stuck in gridlock. Loaded with love, compassion, and care, mother was able to negotiate peace between warring factions. This is one reason she was beloved by many.

This love was especially evident growing up. In times when her health wasn't the best, she still made sure my brother and I were involved in activities like piano and karate. Never once did I hear her complain about her lot in life. She never lived or spoke in such a way that made me doubt her love. This is why my love for her was great. When I received the news of her diagnosis, my world rocked inside out and never returned to the place it'd been.

THE WORST DAY OF MY LIFE

I didn't realized how deep my feelings were for my mom until the day she shared her diagnosis. That day, in an instant, my world was broken. Before the phone call, life was uneventful: a doctoral student, single, hoping to find love and hopeful of a future career. But suddenly, life turned one hundred and eighty degrees. Mother called and told me the news. To date, those words are the worst words I've ever received in life. "I'm dying, please come and be with me," she said. My heart sank in despair. All I remember doing the rest of the day is sitting in a chair, crying, praying, sleeping and listening to Christian music. Never before had I felt so morose and helpless. Depression weighed like an anvil.

The next day, getting out of bed was difficult; the weight of the pain kept pressing me down.[1] A personal voyage of a "dark night of the soul" began—a period where the soul experiences gloom for the purpose of cleansing.[2] Mother's phone call marked the first day of the most pain-filled part of my life journey so far. I felt in my heart things I'd never before experienced.

The journey of the heart takes many roads. Some roads lead to love, pleasure, accomplishment, or success. Other roads take darker turns of pain, affliction, tragedy, illness, or loss. We prefer more pleasant roads, but the journey of the heart always encompasses darker turns along the way. My life had now taken that darker turn. The long journey of seeking, searching and changing began.

LEAVING MY LIFE

Soon after the news, I boarded a plane from Ohio to California to be with mom. One thought dominated my mind; I need to get people praying.

I got off the plane and went to mom's house. Greeted by mom's big smile, strong heart, and zestful spirit, it was as if nothing unusual was happening to her. Mom wasn't depressed or feeling sorry for herself. She told me she didn't cry at all and communicated that she wasn't scared. To top it off, her appearance was radiant.

I was given instructions not to cry. I tried my best not to tear up in front of her. However, at night and when she wasn't around, crying was natural. Tears poured from my heart. I don't cry much and have actually gone years without crying, but at the start of this journey, tears suddenly became a common companion.

Time with loved ones, I believe, is our most precious commodity and currency. No greater asset exists. But, time with loved ones wasn't always on my mind—I was. When life had little turmoil, I often thought selfishly. Only now did I realize the treasure of time. As I looked in my beautiful mother's face and realized that time was limited, life's purpose became clear. I needed to make the most of every moment we had left together. And so, the journey of suffering began as I supported mom in her fight against cancer. This journey allowed my soul to grow.[3]

IN GOD'S HANDS

God's unexpected plan offered my soul two things: comfort and hope. Though turmoil often seemed too much for my mind and heart, God used situations I experienced to mold me. As believers and disciples of Jesus, we realize that the ultimate burden of responsibility for pain is with God. We make choices, but God lives, works and takes the burden of responsibility in it all.

Pilate, blind to his own limits and clouded by his authoritative position, stated to Jesus, "You will not speak to me? Do you not know that I have authority to release you and authority to crucify you?"[4] Pilate had no real say. Jesus rightly responded, "You would have no authority over me at all unless it had been given to you from above."[5] Power resided in God, not Pilate. The governor of Judea didn't realize he was God's resource moved along by a bigger plan.

Jesus provides the example to deal with our "personal Pilates".[6] These Pilates are required components God uses to mold his children, but we're not a fatality of the components' wills, stances, or resolutions any more than Christ was a simple, injured party of Pilate. Jesus said, "I have said these things to you, that in me you may have peace. In this world you will have trouble. But take heart; I have overcome the world."[7]

Economic wealth, health, or peaceful circumstances aren't guaranteed. Life's difficulties don't need to create fear. We have safety within God's plans and resources even if eyes can't see.

GOOD OUT OF BAD

Despite all of the trials, afflictions, tears and sorrow, good comes through each part of our journey. This book looks into my "Journey of Tears" theology.[8] Tears poured from the heart almost every day. This part of my life taught me that love is pleasant. Yet, sometimes, it's also painful, and this kind of pain is good pain. Life without certain types of pain can mean a life without knowing deeper love. I cried so much throughout this part of the journey, and experienced great pain because I grew in learning how to love more deeply. It was pain worth taking.

THE GIFT OF PRAYING WITH A LOVED ONE

The book's title, "Praying with Mom," arose from that unique time with my mother almost every night before bed that we prayed together. Those times offered opportunity to know mom in ways I never had. Before mom was diagnosed we prayed together maybe a handful of times. After her diagnosis prayer became common, something precious that I cherished. As painful as it was to experience mom with cancer, memories I keep from our times of praying bring sweetness to my heart. Her words uttered to God back then came from childlike faith, which stored up cherished memories for me now.

GOD'S WAYS ARE HIGHER THAN MINE

Sometimes God's leading is clear and easy to follow, like Israel following the cloud by day and the ball of fire by night.[9] Other times, God's leading is more silent and obscure to us.[10] Our path is uncertain. We may have no notion where we're headed. We only know that God is leading and can be trusted. The author of Lamentations writes, "He has walled me in so that I can't escape; he has made my chains heavy; though I call and cry for help, he shuts out my prayer; he has blocked my ways with blocks of stones; he has made my paths crooked."[11] Silence can be a tool of God's testing and molding.

For me, the silent method felt cruel, left me thinking I was unloved by God. Pride demanded I understand and have a say in everything happening. But, if human understanding is necessary to make God's case then he isn't mighty, sovereign or all-powerful. There are aspects of our journey and aspects of God's creation that we can know and understand, but our knowledge and ability to understand takes us only so far. There are always aspects beyond our grasp. This is where faith replaces knowledge, and trust replaces understanding. Secret things belong to our God.[12] We won't know everything about our life's journey, and even if God tried to explain it to us, we likely wouldn't understand.[13] He promises to guide us and lead us in ways that are good, perfect and acceptable if we walk as a living offering.[14] The truth of his presence, guidance and leading in my journey authored my peace of mind and calmness for my heart.[15]

ENDNOTES

1. If not for the phone call of a friend from England, I doubt I would have had the strength to get out of bed that day.
2. See John of the Cross "The Dark Night of the Soul." By Bridge-Logos Publishers.
3. Philippians 3:10.
4. John 19:10.

5. John 19:11.
6. I believe this thought was inspired by the devotional "Daily With the King" or "My Utmost for His Highest." These two devotionals were very influential and some of their thoughts may be expressed in the coming pages.
7. John 16:33.
8. Psalm 56:8.
9. See Exodus 13:21.
10. See Psalm 22; Psalm 88:18, Ruth 1.
11. Lamentations 3:7–9.
12. Deut. 29:29.
13. See Job 38–42.
14. Romans 12:1–2.
15. Psalm 16:8–9.

2

Unbelief

And without faith it is impossible to please him,
for whoever would draw near to God must believe that he exists and that he rewards those who seek him.

—Hebrews 11:6

The beginning of anxiety is the end of faith,
and the beginning of true faith is the end of anxiety.

—George E Mueller

From 2000–2007, the Federal Reserve Bank helped to create an economic bubble. Some economists warned that the bubble would burst and a recession or depression could occur. In July of 2005, when asked about the possibility of a bursting economic bubble or recession and a decline in housing, Ben Bernancke felt it would be unlikely.[1] Bernancke was wrong. The bubble burst. In some places housing prices declined over 50 percent, and a devastating recession immediately hit. Bernancke wasn't a victim of lack of knowledge, poor intelligence or even bad information; his data was the same as those warning of potential trouble. He just didn't think or believe such things could and would happen. An incorrect belief system always leads to a reality of harsh consequences.

Unbelief

This is also true in spiritual matters. Many people hold the world view that what I believe is true for me and what you believe is true for you. Each person holds their own belief, and everyone is fine. Beliefs have consequences and false beliefs, no matter how well intentioned, lead to calamity. A.W. Tozer said, "Unbelief is actually perverted faith, for it puts its trust not in the living God but in dying men."[2]

REORGANIZATION OF BELIEFS

Often, in times of suffering, belief systems get reorganized. People, institutions, economies and philosophical systems that were once foundations of thinking get abandoned. Newer ones providing less pain are adopted.

During mom's illness one of my biggest struggles that God revealed was a lack of faith. The second largest struggle was pride in my heart.[3] Pride over glorifies an individual and under glorifies God.[4] It shares brother and sisterhood with unbelief. Horatius Bonar writes, "In all unbelief there are these two things: a good opinion of one's self, and a bad opinion of God."[5] In my head, I always hoped I was a humble person. Through mom's experience with cancer God showed me that my heart was far from where it needed to be.

Suffering is one antidote against poisonous pride. William Gurnall, a great Puritan thinker, wrote, "When men stand high their heads do not grow dizzy till they look down; when men look down upon those that are worse than themselves, or less holy than themselves, then their heads turn round; looking up would cure this disease. The most holy men, when once they have fixed their eyes awhile upon God's holiness and then looked upon themselves, have been quite out of love with themselves."[6] Suffering has a way of accomplishing what Gurnall suggests. It turns our focus back toward God and mirrors a more realistic reflection of who we truly are. For me, clearer focus was about to be aligned. Suffering would be the tool used to correct me.[7] At the time, I studied at a British school, but real education started one week before my mother told me her circumstances.

THE JOURNEY BEGINS

It was a dark, chilly evening in England. Nighttime fell by 4 with no hint of light. It could easily pass as midnight in the US. One person at the school suddenly became terribly ill. Hunched over in great pain, wincing constantly with barely enough strength to stand, talk and breathe, I watched. Fortunately, another student was also a practicing physician and able to examine him. His diagnosis: stones. "Get him to the hospital," uttered the physician. The ill man got up, walking with great difficulty due to the pain. He went to the hospital after barely making it to the car.

What do people that are training to serve God do when trouble arises? They pray. This schoolmate's pain was where God began to reveal I was the owner of a prideful, unbelieving heart. One of the ladies gathered us together like a hen gathering its chicks. We all huddled together as one group to pray. The first thought that came to me was, "This won't help him at all; it's not going to do any good." Another thought in my head was, "This is a waste of time." I read many times in many sections of the Gospels where Jesus healed, but I didn't think Jesus healed in today's world or in my environment.

My unbelief may also have been rooted in self-protection where fear to take risk exists. I know that if the outcome doesn't correspond with the original desire or intent, hurt arises. Maybe in my heart, I didn't want to be disappointed if I prayed for healing and it never happened. I had no problem saying the phrase, "God *can* heal" in my head, but that night I realized I hadn't accepted and believed it to be true within my heart that he *would*. Maybe I didn't believe in healing because I'd never seen anyone healed by prayer. Maybe I was hardened by my prideful attitude toward Charismatic and Pentecostal brothers and sisters that believe in healing and have this aspect woven in the fabric of their theology. John Stott writes, "Unbelief is not a misfortune to be pitied; it is a sin to be deplored. Its sinfulness lies in the fact that it contradicts the word of the one, true God and thus attributes falsehood to him."[8] I believed in my head that God *could* heal, but in my heart I didn't think he *would*. God began working change in all of that.

MY FIRST HEALING PRAYER EXPERIENCE

The next day I saw the ill man from the previous night, now completely recovered. In fact, the hospital said that there was nothing wrong with him. I said to myself, "I saw him the night before. He was so ill that he was hunched over in the bathroom, in great pain, barely able to walk.

Another physician already diagnosed him with stones." Yet, there he was as if nothing ever happened to him. It was the first person healed that I'd ever met. God showed me that I needed to repent. I felt like the father in Mark 9:14-29, ". . . help me with my unbelief."[9] Without my knowing, God was preparing me for the challenge ahead, because this happened about a week before mom called with the news that changed my life forever.

I soon returned to the USA and began writing the Christmas sermon. My prayer was that God would give me something new in the message, something I never previously noticed. I studied the section in Luke 1:5-79 when the angel, Gabriel, visited both Zechariah and Mary. Zechariah, an older scholar of the ancient Torah and well respected priest in the community who knew Scriptures thoroughly and obeyed, when visited by Gabriel didn't believe. Mary, on the other hand, was likely about age 13, only a teenager by today's standard. Women weren't allowed to learn the Scriptures the same way men could in the days of Christ, so Mary's knowledge of the Torah—Holy Scripture—was minimal at best. When Gabriel visited each of them, Mary believed, but Zechariah didn't. See? Faith isn't entirely dependent on age or knowledge. The condition of the heart and humility are much better gauges. God showed me that I was like Zechariah.

MARY FAITH

My mother's sweet and childlike faith reminded me of the kind of "Mary Faith" that God honored. I remember once our dog ran away and my mother and I together with some neighborhood children drove around looking for him. I remember my mom asked the children in the back seat to pray that our dog would return. At the time, I was studying for my Masters of Divinity, a degree many ministers obtain, but again, my unbelief manifested in spite of what I'd been studying. The main thought in my mind? "Mom, this is silly." I turned out to be the silly one, because before the prayer finished the dog came running toward the car.

My mother often demonstrated this type of faith. If she lost something, she prayed and often God helped her find it. She prayed over things that many of us don't think to pray, and often God answered her. I imagine God loves simple, innocent faith that trusts, believes, and is expressed through interaction with him.

Praying with Mom

Prayer depends on God, and a life without prayer is a life of self-dependence. The great saints of old were often men and women of prayer. I wasn't like them. Charles Spurgeon said, "Prayer pulls the rope below and the great bell rings above in the ears of God. Some scarcely stir the bell, for they pray languidly. Others give an occasional pluck at the rope, but he who wins with heaven is the man who grasps the rope boldly and pulls continuously, with all his might."[10] My prayer life was about to change.

Unbelief doesn't just strike during big events. Unbelief manifests in many forms. Jesus often asks us where he fits into our everyday life. The choices we make—from what books to read, which relationships to invest in, how to use our time and money—all reflect whether or not we truly believe. When other things take first place in our heart, disorder emerges. Jesus taught us, "Do not be anxious about your life, what you will eat or what you will drink, nor about your body, what you will put on. Isn't life more than food, and the body more than clothing? And which of you by being anxious can add a single hour to his span of life?"[11] Worry indicates that we don't trust God to provide for our life. The practical details of life—money, retirement, supporting a family, finding the right job, what clothes to buy and wear—are details that can lead to worry and unbelief.

The Gospel of Matthew teaches us that the cares and worries of the world are things that prevent growth.[12] Human nature has difficulty trusting what we can't see, but it's precisely the depending vision of the Lord that roots faith.[13] Intentionally discarding selfish ambition and busy-ness while surrendering and obeying God's Word all cure us of distrust and self-dependence.

God used my own sermon to test whether I'd discard my own ambition and trust him with my life. After I shared the message from the lives of Zechariah and Mary, my heart convinced my mind that I was a Zechariah. I needed help to believe God and all that's unseen. My mind kept telling me I needed simpler faith like my mother's. Little did I realize that within days I'd be with my mom enrolling in her school.

On Christmas evening at 11:30, about twelve hours after sharing the Christmas message, my brother called and told me the news. Shock struck, but it didn't fully hit me until the next day when mom called herself. The pain in my heart was the greatest pain I'd ever felt.

ENDNOTES

1. Interview in July 2005, CNBC. See also http://www.youtube.com/watch?v=HQ79Pt2GNJo.
2. http://www.pietyhilldesign.com/gcq/quotepages/unbelief.html
3. Chapter 9 will go more deeply into the issue of pride but its struggle leaves shadows in other chapters.
4. Psalm 10:4.
5. Most of the quotes in this work will be taken from the website: www.pietyhilldesign.com.
6. www.pietyhilldesign.com.
7. Romans 5:3–5.
8. http://www.pietyhilldesign.com/gcq/quotepages/unbelief.html.
9. Mark 9:24.
10. http://www.pietyhilldesign.com/gcq/quotepages/prayer.html.
11. Matthew 6:25, 27.
12. Matthew 13:22.
13. Hebrews 11:1.

3

Pain

"For I am ready to fall, and my pain is ever before me."
—Psalm 38:17

"Tribulations cannot cease until God either sees us remade or sees our remaking is now hopeless."
—C.S. Lewis

British author George MacDonald said, "All misery is God unknown." George wasn't as well known as his contemporaries. Lewis Carroll (*Alice in Wonderland*), Alfred Tennyson, Charles Dickens, and Walt Whitman are much more recognizable. His style of using imagination and fantasy to describe the state of the human heart highly influenced notable authors C.S. Lewis (*Narnia*) and J.R.R. Tolkien (*The Lord of the Rings*). C.S. Lewis once said, "I have never concealed the fact that I regard him as my master; indeed I fancy I have never written a book in which I did not quote from George."[1]

MacDonald's work, *A Rough Shacking*, tells the story of an 1887 earthquake, which violently affected his home on the Italian Mediterranean coast. MacDonald writes words that sear our consciousness in understanding pain: "We are so full of ourselves, and feel so grand, that we should never come to know what poor creatures we are, never begin to do better, but for the knock-down blows that the loving God gives us. We do not like them, but He does not spare us."[2] Pain is one of God's tools that reveal his love for us. In experiencing pain God roots out evil and immaturity, replanting in our hearts the character of Christ. MacDonald expresses similar thoughts in his poem, "The Giver".

> To give a thing and take again
> Is counted meanness among men;
> To take away what once was given
> Cannot then be the way of heaven!
> But human hearts are crumbly stuff,
> And never, never love enough,
> Therefore God takes and, with a smile,
> Puts our best things away a while.
> Thereon some weep, some rave, some scorn,
> Some wish they never had been born:
> Some humble grow at last and still,
> And God gives them what they will.[3]

PAINFUL BEGINNING

My initial reaction to mother's diagnosis was a sudden shock that didn't fully sink in. The news struck, but the brunt of the pain came the next day when mother personally shared the news via telephone. It was a direct blow more crushing than any news I'd ever received. After hanging up the phone, tears began to fall in waves that didn't cease. All I remember about the day my mother first told me is crying, sitting, sleeping and listening to Christian music on the radio. The most painful period of my life had begun, and it seemed I'd be crying a lifetime of tears.

Maybe tears were many because of father's death at only nine years old. Maybe it was unresolved grief. On a business trip in San Diego dad had gone swimming alone. The sea took his life as he drowned in a rip current. Losing him at such a young age was difficult, but time helped heal the wound. Maybe my mourning for him had never finished.

As a young boy at age 9, my first news from mom was that dad was missing. It wasn't easy to comprehend. As time passed and no news from father came, tension in me mounted and what was once not easy to understand suddenly became clear, dad was gone. I still remember the day he was to arrive home from his business trip. I went to the front porch of our house and told myself that I wasn't leaving until dad came back. He never came. The next morning I rushed to his study to see if he'd arrived late while I slept. The study was empty. Only later, after mom returned from San Diego where my father was on a business trip, did I finally understand. Mother told me that my father was dead and that he'd drowned in a rip current. I'll never forget that day. It was, until mom's news, the saddest day of my life. News of mom's condition was worse than news of dad's death. There's an emotional naivety possessed at age 9 that I no longer had as an adult. Regardless of the psychology or any delayed emotional condition in my situation, I knew the difficulty was rooted in loving my mother and not wanting her to go. The doctor estimated four months for her to live without treatment and seven to twelve months to live with it. Time with my mom could be short.[4]

A BRIEF HOPE

One song by Philips, Craig and Dean gave me a moment to hope. It still moves me when I hear it. "You Are God Alone" played, and for a brief moment despair left me. Focus shifted away from my mom and me and onto God. The chorus of the song seared my soul with momentary respite from the anguish and infused optimism that mom would be fine. The contents of the chorus reminded me that God was in control and on the throne and that He is God.

For a brief moment in time, the turmoil and tears ceased, and comfort and hope renewed. Everything I ever learned or believed about God would soon be tested. Mother needed prayer, so I sent out the following email.[5] It was the first of many.

> *Dear brothers and sisters in Christ,*
> *I received a call from my mother informing me that she has lung cancer. It's in late stages as it wasn't detected during my mother's regular doctor check-ups. Her prognosis is unsure. She could have a few months to a long life depending on how she responds to treatment. I'll move out there soon to help her with her treatment and be out there indefinitely. Please pray for her that God can heal her and do a miracle. In times like this I rest in God's sovereignty, knowing that my mom is a believer and has peace as well.*
> *Trusting him,*
> *Mike*

My mother was diagnosed with stage 4 lung cancer which is the highest stage of diagnosis. Regardless of its stage, lung cancer has a high mortality rate. Over 50 percent of people diagnosed with lung cancer die within a year. The situation was dire. The only one that could pull us out was God.

THE FRIENDSHIP OF PAIN

I don't recall a time in my life when I was in as much pain. Depression's anvil was so heavy. It weighed me down in bed the day after my mother's call. So heavy was its weight, I felt no strength to rise from my mattress. All I could do was lay staring at the ceiling, sobbing uncontrollably. Fortunately, a friend read the email I sent and called long distance from England to bridge the gap. Without that call I likely would've been in bed the whole day. Only after I hung up the phone did I muster the strength to get up.

The body of Christ is crucial in times of discouragement and desperation. Just like our physical body releases defense and protection when sickness and injury come, the spiritual body releases ministry in order to prevent drying up.[6] Blood cells physically attack foreign intruders. The body of Christ comes to aid, protect and defend those that are spiritually and emotionally hurting.

REFLECTION

Armed with prayer, I spent the majority of my time in California with my mother. Time passed, and mom did well. The first year was hard. The brightest news was that my mom lived. Mother not only lived through the first year, she seemed to get better. I believe because of prayer.[7] We would go to the oncologist's office for reports. They were often positive reports: stable or shrinkage. There were times when the doctor reported growth which caused my spirit to be low, but for the most part, our first year was filled with good news and hope that her time on earth wasn't finished. It was an emotional roller coaster, but I was happy to ride it if it meant my mom lived.

As I reflect on the time, I realize pain was my friend. To experience great love is to experience great pain. It was hard to weep so much and be in such pain, but behind the tears was a deep love for my mother. Cancer revealed the great love in my heart for her. The value of pain caused by love far exceeds the worst pain we humans can experience, no love. Nothing is emptier. Pain showed the degree of love that resided in my heart for mom, more than I ever imagined. Hurt came because of the amount that existed, not a lack of it. Dr. Paul Brand writes, "Pain truly is the gift nobody wants."[8] I didn't want to befriend pain, but it fertilized the garden of my spirit. Through the hurt, my soul grew. I saw unpleasant things living and growing inside myself that forced me to grow more in the identity of my Savior's deep love.

People strive for satisfaction in many ways: money, fame, prestige, and approval. We seek titles, accolades, relationships, possessions and pleasure, but the only thing that truly satisfies is love. Pain is a gift? Yes. It measures how much love our life holds. A life with little love equals a life with little satisfaction. Only those that love are satisfied.

I believe this innate desire to feel important and find satisfaction is something inborn. Children instinctively long to be loved. It doesn't dissipate over time and growth, but it manifests itself in different ways throughout our life journey. Is it the root of many strivings and desires? I don't have the answer. I do know the answer to what I prayed for in regards to mom's circumstances: a miracle.

Augustine wrote in his *Confessions* that, "Everywhere a greater joy is preceded by a greater suffering."[9] To be a living disciple of Christ means to know pain. There's great joy in experiencing the resurrection power of Christ, but to follow him also means to fellowship with him through suffering.[10]

Happiness in the midst of difficulty can be part of the Christian experience. We read the letter to the Philippians and see Paul filled with joy, but this isn't the full experience. Pain participated. Paul experienced pain in prison and under house arrest; his difficult circumstances didn't rob him of the joy in following Christ. He had his mind on the return of Christ and fellow believers' needs.[11] His mind focused on the eternal, heavenly realm.[12] Mundane concerns of the world weren't part of his thought life.

Many believers in Christ grow dim and dejected during times of pain. In order to transform from a natural person to a spiritual one, pain usually must be experienced. I imagine a caterpillar when metamorphosing into a butterfly endures excruciating pain when trying to break free from that cocoon, ultimately emerging as a beautiful butterfly. Remove the process, deny the caterpillar the pain of freeing itself from the cocoon and metamorphosis becomes incomplete, and the beautiful butterfly likely doesn't survive or at least can't fly. Pascal felt that the reason believers experienced pain was due to moral filth residing in our heart and soul. To resist pain would actually bring about more pain.

Many who claim to love and follow Christ experience needless pain because they don't want to endure trials brought into their life that produce in their soul the beauty and genuine life of Christ. Human nature desires comfort and effortlessness due to false expectations of what learning to live and grow in character really means. Jesus didn't come to make us feel good but to *be* and *do* good (more specifically righteous). A believer who endures the pain of discipleship often forsakes comfort and ease in the world.

True triumph often comes through pain. Muscles in the body break down after weight training, yet ultimately rebuild more muscle mass. God's activity in our life through his spirit works to break down imperfections and heal us through a greater desire for trusting and knowing him. Much intimacy with Christ is experienced through pain. First Peter 5:10–11 says, "after you have suffered a little while, the God of all grace, who has called you to his eternal glory in Christ, will himself restore, confirm, strengthen, and establish you. To him be the dominion forever and ever. Amen." May we all be good students during God's lessons from pain. I enrolled. Though I didn't seek or want to experience hurt, my heart needed its lessons in order to grow. Being a disciple of Jesus meant fellowshipping with him through some suffering. This step was non-negotiable.

ENDNOTES

1. See D.L. Neuhouser *George MacDonald* (USA: Victor Books, 1990). MacDonald did posses controversial theological positions, e.g. animals in heaven, not adhering to the substitutionary atonement. But his contribution to understanding the human soul and spirit should not be discarded.
2. G. MacDonald *A Rough Shacking* (London: Blackie and Son, Limited, 1890) p.152. I am indebted to D.L. Neuhouser's work cited above. His thorough research has allowed people like me to enjoy the breadth of MacDonald's thought and work. Much of the citations to MacDonald were guided by his previous book.
3. G. MacDonald *Poetical Works Volume II* (London: Chatto and Windus, 1911) p.128.
4. One thing I have learned during this trying time is that though doctors do a good job, they are fallible and human. Not only are second opinions necessary but careful research should be done by family members. There are a lot of treatment options out there and people doing research that other doctors would not be aware of. Finding as much knowledge and information is crucial.
5. Emails in the book may have been modified from their original form.
6. Thanks also goes out to my friend Greg Brown, who met with me that day, had lunch and was able to make me laugh even though it was the worst day of my life.
7. 2 Corinthian 1:11
8. : Yancey, P., *Where is God When it Hurts* (Grand Rapids: Zondervan, 1997) 20.
9. Confessions can be read online, one site is: http://www.stoa.org/hippo/.
10. Phil. 3:10–11.
11. Phil.1:3–6,10.
12. Col. 3:1–2.

4

Providence

Our God is in the heavens; he does all that he pleases.
—Psalm 115:3

So great and boundless is God's wisdom
that he knows right well how to use evil instruments to do good.
—John Calvin

THE AENEID, AN EPIC poem written by Vergil, Publius Vergilius Maro, was produced around 19 BC and gives an account of Rome's beginning. Vergil was present when Rome transformed from a hectic Republic to an Empire that would dominate the world. The differentiation between myth and fact wasn't prominent during Vergil's time, so his epic served two purposes: to record history and tell a story.

Aeneas, the main character of *The Aeneid*, is likely analogous to Augustus, the founder of the Roman Empire.[1] After the sacking of Troy by the Greeks during the Trojan War, Aeneas, a survivor of the Trojan horse invasion, embarks on a seven-year journey to establish a new life for the Trojans. The story begins with Aeneas and his followers shipwrecked in Carthage. Throughout the seven years, challenges prevent them from their goal of founding Rome. Without the gods helping Aeneas, Rome wouldn't exist.

But not all of the gods share in the plan to help Aeneas. Juno, who loves Carthage and knows Aeneas will conquer her beloved city, tries to prevent his success. The future Romans experience Juno's harsh storms, one which forces Aeneas into a cave with a highly passionate, beautiful woman, the queen of Carthage. Dido is her name, and she's in love with Aeneas. Juno hopes the beauty and love of Dido will captivate Aeneas' heart and thwart his pursuit of founding Rome. Juno's plot fails. Aeneas wouldn't forsake his mission for Dido. When Dido discovers Aeneas has gone, she commits suicide. The light from her funeral aids the travelers on their voyage out of Carthage.

Throughout the poem—divided into 12 books—the Trojans endure various situations, mainly caused by conflict with the gods. In the final scene Aeneas kills Turnus, a war hero from an area near Latimus, which became the city where the Trojans settled. Juno and Jupiter, the queen and king of the gods, agree that Aeneas will win the duel, but the Trojans mustn't continue to practice their previous mores and become Latin in language and culture.

The *Aeneid* is a good illustration of providential work.[2] While humanity experiences all sorts of trials and challenges, the gods control, unbeknownst to the humans. Juno tried desperately to stop Rome's founding, but nothing hindered the ultimate plan of Jupiter, king of the gods.

BIBLICAL PROVIDENCE

Christianity holds the doctrine of providence. Jonathan Edwards, the great American theologian, considered providence one of the sweetest doctrines of the Christian church. Indeed, when life attacks with difficulties, the doctrine of providence can be a soft cushion. Unlike the Roman gods, Yahweh—God—isn't fickle, and his plan is already in motion. He doesn't have to worry about a Juno. Even Satan is a mere tool in his hand.

PROVIDENCE AS GOOD MEDICINE
FOR THE HURTING HEART

Affliction is part of life; its pangs assault the heart. No human being is immune. Few people continue as normal when life events press down. Hardship and trials test whether a person truly believes and loves God.

One pillar in Reformed theology is the steadfast, uncompromising belief in God's sovereignty and providence. Providence is defined as: "the foreseeing care and guidance of God or nature over the creatures of the earth. God, especially when conceived as omnisciently directing the universe and the affairs of humankind with wise benevolence, a manifestation of divine care or direction."[6]

Sovereignty, a related word or synonym and often used in the same context, is defined as: "of God, his absolute right to do all things according to his own good pleasure (Dan. 4:25, 35; Rom. 9:15–23; 1 Tim. 6:15; Rev. 4:11)."[7]

Sovereignty should be one of the most cherished doctrines in Christian faith, lighting faith's pathway. When life's dreams shatter and our life's circumstances turn painful, Sovereignty anchors our expectation that nothing extends outside God's grasp. He's in control. Nothing happens to us that God doesn't either cause or allow; therefore, we can have absolute faith that pain can turn to joy and that God can use hardship for good. He won't waste our afflictions.[8] His character and nature are the defining mark for all that's good, so we trust this being that controls everything. We trust his goodness. This is why providence is a cornerstone of our belief. It gives glory to God and peace to our souls, because a good and loving God holds ultimate responsibility for all that is and all that happens. Times of affliction test whether people truly live out their belief of this doctrine. I always cherished these doctrines, but as circumstances in my life altered God used this trial alongside my mom to see if I really wanted to live them.

When life crumbles, the examples from saints of old help us. Those before us endured trials by holding to their good, faithful God. One example was Horatio G. Spafford.[9] The Great Chicago fire of 1871 instantly put Spafford in financial ruin. His business and fortune were gone, eaten away by fire. Not long after, Spafford's wife and four daughters boarded a ship to cross the Atlantic. Tragically, the ship crashed into another and sank. Spafford's wife survived, but his four daughters didn't. Spafford later boarded a ship to be with his wife. Rather than resenting God who had the power and ability to save his daughters and his business yet didn't, Spafford responded in faith, trusting that God had a plan. As Spafford's ship neared the spot where his daughters died, God filled his heart with the now famous hymn, "It is Well with My Soul".

Praying with Mom

> When peace, like a river, attendeth my way
> When sorrows like sea billows roll;
> Whatever my lot, Thou has taught me to say
> It is well, it is well, with my soul.
> Refrain
> It is well, with my soul
> It is well, with my soul
> It is well, it is well, with my soul.
> Though Satan should buffet, though trials should come
> Let this blest assurance control
> That Christ has regarded my helpless estate
> And hath shed his own blood for my soul.
> Refrain
> My sin, oh, the bliss of this glorious thought!
> My sin, not in part but the whole
> Is nailed to the cross, and I bear it no more
> Praise the Lord, praise the Lord, o my soul!
> Refrain
> For me, be it Christ, be it Christ hence to live:
> If Jordan above me shall roll
> No pang shall be mine, for in death as in life
> Thou wilt whisper Thy peace to my soul.
> Refrain
> But, Lord, 'tis for Thee, for Thy coming we wait
> The sky, not the grave, is our goal;
> Oh trump of the angel! Oh voice of the Lord!
> Blessèd hope, blessèd rest of my soul!
> Refrain
> And Lord, haste the day when my faith shall be sight
> The clouds be rolled back as a scroll;
> The trump shall resound, and the Lord shall descend
> Even so, it is well with my soul.
> Refrain

Every circumstance surrounding Spafford should've led to resentment and hatred toward God. His faith should've been shattered. It wasn't. To Spafford, God was bigger than circumstances, and he believed that tragedy could someday turn to triumph.

There were many times in my life that I was mad at God. I remember driving alone and yelling at God in the car. It was maybe six months into mother's illness. I was in the car by myself when I suddenly screamed, "You're supposed to be sovereign, if you're so powerful, then why don't you just heal my mom now?!"

Providence

A mentor of mine lost his wife of forty years and told me that one time he left his car, went into the woods and just shouted from the top of his lungs. I took this time to do my own shouting at God. I didn't like the hurt I was experiencing. I wanted to see my mom healthy. Although she was stable most of the time, I wanted the miracle God wasn't giving. Driving down the small street in California yelling—in the otherwise silence of my car—proved to be therapeutic. I held nothing back.

Regardless of my circumstance, I needed the faith of Spafford. Why should God be my scapegoat? He'd already sent Christ to come and appease the wrath of sin. Christ will come again to finish the job. Yet, painful reminders of our world being so imperfect led to my anger and shouts at God which had actually made my heart feel better. Thankfully, looking back, I realize God could take it. John Flavel wrote, "Sometimes providences, like Hebrew letters, must be read backward." My circumstances weren't as devastating as a saint like Spafford's, and definitely not as numerous as Job's. But, my hurt was real, all the same.

Job, what a good example in times of distress! Losing his wealth, health and children, the Bible says God felt that Job wouldn't renounce his faith, so he allowed Satan to test Job. The adversary challenged God saying that the only reason Job was righteous was because he was being blessed by the hand of the Almighty. The adversary believed he could entice Job to renounce his faith if he was allowed to subject Job to affliction instead of blessing. God knew Job's heart and allowed him to be tested. The adversary took away almost everything. Job's wife even encouraged her husband to give up and just die. But the true substance in Job's heart wasn't his love of wealth, health or family. At the heart of his life was devout faith and love for God that allowed him candidacy for such a strong adversarial test. Job passed. The adversary was defeated, and God was glorified.

Job demanded what many of us demand when we experience trials and afflictions in life: answers. No direct answer was given, except one: God himself. He reminded Job of the glory and grandeur of his Lord. Job found comfort and strength to endure the tests. God's sovereignty sees us through the challenges and storms of life.[10]

Afterward, Job had no more questions. Were God to grant his presence as my audience like he did Job, I believe God would've responded similarly to my shouts. But, unlike Job, I probably wouldn't have been able to handle the presence of God and live.[11]

Praying with Mom

Difficult times shouldn't surprise us, but they often do. Sometimes when life is going well a sudden crisis brings much shock and strain. The Bible says this world has much trouble, but Christ has overcome it.[12] The Psalms display this, for example, Ps. 13:1-2 "How long, O LORD? Will you forget me forever? How long will you hide your face from me? 2 How long must I take counsel in my soul and have sorrow in my heart all the day? How long shall my enemy be exalted over me?" The psalmist is open about the pain and struggle. In personal struggle many of us believe we need to cover the struggle up and not display our weakness. Psalm 13 is an example that struggle is common to life and is acceptable to share with others.

Later in the psalm, there's a change of the heart's condition. A display of peace and rest is exhibited in the psalmist rather than sorrow. Psalm 13:5-6: "But I have trusted in your steadfast love; my heart shall rejoice in your salvation. I will sing to the LORD, because he has dealt bountifully with me." Did the psalmist's circumstance change? Most likely no, but the attitude of the psalmist's heart changed. And, despite the difficult circumstances, the heart began to reflect rest and peace instead of sorrow and pain.

During hard times, providence becomes one of the sweetest things. Trusting in an all powerful God can bring hope in the midst of despair. The providence of God became a sweet doctrine to me as I trusted God with my mom's health. I doubt my mother could ever give a theological treatise on providence, but I know a treatise isn't required in order to live or believe in it. My mother's prayers were filled with a belief that God could heal her, and also a belief that if he didn't, that was ok. I knew in my heart that for God to answer my prayers for mom's healing would actually be the lesser experience of the two possibilities for her—because to be with Jesus is so much better than imperfect bodies in an imperfect world.[13] In my heart I was selfish and didn't want her with Jesus yet, so I continued to pray for God to heal mom and continued asking others to join in prayer.[14]

My mother always began prayer with "beloved heavenly Father" and asked God to use the chemotherapy to kill off all of the cancer. She often prayed about her life circumstances. If she wronged someone, she asked forgiveness. If someone else was in distress, we prayed for the person. Along the way we met many people battling cancer. We prayed for their healing too. We'd pray for our families, friends and thank God for all that he gave us. Most of all, I loved listening to mom's child-like faith accompanied by the surrendered faith that God had the best in mind for us all. I cherished prayer with my mom. They were some of the sweetest times of life so far that remain sweet today.

I took Luke 18:1 literally and prayed constantly for mom. Often, I knelt down at night by her bedroom door and poured out my heart to God inside my soul asking him to heal her. I cried pools of tears at that doorway, all prayers of love.

Faith's vast training ground stretches out within the reality of life. God allows us to experience ruin and barrenness alongside abundant beauty. Sometimes it seems as if God abandons us. He seems silent when we need him to speak. Humankind rarely or willingly chooses this. In fact, our life is often filled with self-protective walls against such silence or abandonment. But God's way leads us through occasional dark nights of the soul. Young believers' faith grows through blessings, answered prayer, exciting experiences and happy feelings. Journeying along in faith though often means we face barrenness and ruin at some points along our path. The Lord leads us to new heights with him, and once we arrive we realize that the sweetness of our relationship with him grew sweeter during the climbs and descents. The journey takes time. Mother Teresa struggled over thirty years with feeling God was silent. In a letter to Jesus she wrote:

> Lord, my God, who am I that You should forsake me? The child of your love—and now become as the most hated one... You have thrown away as unwanted—unloved... So many unanswered questions live within me afraid to uncover them—because of the blasphemy—If there be a God—please forgive me... I am told that God loves me, and yet the reality of darkness and coldness and emptiness is so great that nothing touches my soul.

On Mother Teresa's struggle and her example of sainthood, Dinesh D'Souza writes:

> But Mother Teresa's heart-wrenching self-examination is entirely familiar to thoughtful Christians. For instance, her insistent theme that she is being forsaken by God recalls Christ's plaintive cry on the cross, "Why have You forsaken me?"...
>
> The greatness of Mother Teresa is that even when she was deprived of the spiritual satisfactions of feeling God's presence in her life, she did not waver, she soldiered on. She was not deterred in her mission. And what she didn't have by way of feeling, she compensated for by way of will. In doing so, she teaches us all something about love: it is not merely a sentiment, to be set aside

when feelings come and go, but rather a decision of the will. That she did what she did in exchange for the love of God is astounding enough. That she did it all even when this love was invisible to her.[16]

The providence of God allows times of barrenness. When we begin to watch for God within our daily life and not regard him as a simple side thought, we see God's patience in forming our character. If we're patient too we can observe the fruit of his providence. This I held onto as I began my journey of purification; or was it, providence that held on to me?

No matter what my head believed, my heart still ached. The journey through the dark night of the soul was a painful one. The soul first breaks down before being built up, which leaves the soul feeling dark and at times dead. Sadness isn't good medicine. We can't be in this state too long or it eats away at our spirit.[17] Providence knows this and helps us along the way.

ENDNOTES

1. See W.J. Campbell's excellent work *The Book of Great Books: A Guide to 100 World Classics* (New York: Fall River Press, 2000) pp.5–6. Many references to the great books will be guided by his insights.

2. I will use sovereignty and providence interchangeably but I will give definitions to both.

3. I will not discuss in detail the issue of Calvinism and Arminianism. For a concise summary as well as a unique synthesis, see http://mediatetheology.org/3_Views.html by Dr. Gordon Olson. His two books *Beyond Calvinism and Arminianism* and *Getting the Gospel Right* are a detailed study of Calvinism and Arminanism through systematic study of Scripture and Theology. He comes to the conclusion of Mediate Theology which is a synthesis of the two positions based on careful exegetical study of the Bible. The best summary I have found on the issue of Calvinism and Arminianism is in Philippians 2:12-13 "Therefore, my beloved, as you have always obeyed, so now, not only as in my presence but much more in my absence, work out your own salvation with fear and trembling, 13 for it is God who works in you, both to will and to work for his good pleasure." Paul asserts God's

working as well as humankind's responsibility in the process.

4. Job 1and 2.
5. Genesis 22:1, 12.
6. Dictionary.com.
7. Easton's Bible Dictionary, accessed on Dictionary.com.
8. Romans 8:28.
9. See also www.cyberhymnal.org.
10. See also Mark 4;35–41.
11. Exodus 19:11–12.
12. John 16:33.
13. Phil. 1:23.
14. 2 Cor. 1:11.
15. "Mother Teresa's Crisis of Faith", by David van Biema, *Time Magazine*, 23 August, 2007
16. Seehttp://townhall.com/columnists/DineshDSouza/2007/09/04/mother_teresa%E2%80%99s_dark_night_of_the_soul. D'Souza is responding to the atheist Christopher Hitchens.
17. Proverbs 13:12.

5

Prayer

> For I know that through your prayers
> and the help of the Spirit of Jesus Christ
> this will turn out for my deliverance.
>
> —Apostle Paul to PHILIPPIANS 1:19

> God expects to hear from you,
> before you can expect to hear from him.
>
> —WILLIAM GURNALL

> Whether we like it or not, asking is the rule of the kingdom.
>
> —CHARLES SPURGEON

STUDYING THE LITERATURE OF the ancient Greeks and Romans, fate is a prominent theme. Prayers uttered to the gods had few—if any—answered. This taught the ancients that prayer was meaningless, because the gods determined everything with no input from humankind. The God of the Bible isn't the same. He's sovereign and in control, but also hears and responds. The Greek verb *akouo*, meaning to hear, is used sixteen times in John's Epistles (*1–2–3 John*). This communicates that our prayers aren't meaningless, audible acts but a way to commune with our Lord. God listens intently to our prayers. Through the eyes of Scripture prayer protects people, prevents God's wrath on friends and ourselves, opens wombs and thwarts military attacks. Indeed, the Bible teaches that prayer matters and is useful in our relationship with God.

A CALL TO PRAYER

When my mother first shared about her condition, she asked me not to tell anyone that she was diagnosed with lung cancer, because she didn't want to burden others. I couldn't honor the request. In fact, instead, I asked her to tell a few people from church so that they could pray. She agreed.

My mother hated adding weight to others' shoulders. Although Paul encouraged people to have a good standing among their social group, it was to be motivated by godly living.[1] Believers in Christ should bear one another's burdens and fulfill the law of Christ.[2] After many tears, mom called a good friend at our home church and asked her to share with a few people so that they could also pray. I began to alert as many people as I could.

I began to read books and Scripture on healing. Throughout the Bible, especially the Gospels, people are healed. Yet, I never internalized these truths in my heart; it was only head knowledge.[3]

Sections on prayer had my attention too. Because the sovereignty of God was such a sweet doctrine to me, the issue of prayer was hard to properly understand. If God does what *he* wants, how is *my* praying relevant? Would prayer be more like what the ancient Greeks and Romans were taught?

Scriptures teach that God responds to prayer.[4] After reading Scripture, I came to the conclusion that God allows us to experience his sovereignty through prayer. In one aspect, he does what he pleases. In other aspects, there's pleasure and communion with us when we pray. This allows us to interact and participate *as* he rules. So, I began to pray constantly for my mother and sought others to pray. I called different churches, and if they reported seeing cancer healed, then I asked them to pray for my mom. A church in Redding, California had a reputation of experiencing cancer healed through prayer.[5] I got on the phone, asked them to pray and later drove my mom to their church to pray for her healing.

Two Scripture passages close to my heart were Luke 18:1 and Matthew 21:21–22 (also found in Mark 11:23–24). Luke 18:1, "And he told

Praying with Mom

them a parable to the effect that they ought always to pray and not lose heart." This verse set the stage for the parable of the persistent widow who continually went before a judge. The judge neither feared God nor man. But the widow constantly asked the judge for justice. He finally gave in because of her persistence. So, I prayed constantly to the Lord, often muttering the phrase "heal my mom" hundreds of times throughout a day.

Jesus' words in Matthew 21:21–22 also played a role in my thinking: "Truly, I say to you, if you have faith and do not doubt, you will not only do what has been done to the fig tree, but even if you say to this mountain, 'Be taken up and thrown into the sea,' it will happen. And whatever you ask in prayer, you will receive, if you have faith." I watched shows like the 700 Club where they prayed using these types of verses. I prayed together with them. I never watched shows like the 700 Club much before, but I knew the show often had stories of people healed. So, now I turned to people like this to teach me. These two verses consistently entered my mind throughout the day.

Every time I came to a passage on prayer in the Bible, I paid particular attention to God's response to prayer accompanied by faith. I began to pray constantly for my mother, trying to believe that she would be healed. I asked many in the body of Christ to do likewise.

At night, when I prayed with my mom, I often felt a sense of comfort and joy to hear mom's prayers. To me she had Mary-like faith. They were simple prayers asking God to heal her so that she could serve Him.

Two other important passages: Philippians 1:19 and 2 Corinthians 1:11. Philippians 1:19 says, ". . . for I know that through your prayers and the help of the Spirit of Jesus Christ this will turn out for my deliverance." Second Corinthians 1:11 states, "You also must help us by prayer, so that many will give thanks on our behalf for the blessing granted us through the prayers of many." The apostle Paul modeled his dependence on prayer and believed the prayers of saints helped him. So, I continued to build my prayer list, scouring the internet for ministries of prayer, calling churches to pray. God led me to individuals who would tell me stories of healing. I quickly sought them out to pray. One great Christian saint greatly desired the prayers of others.[6] His logic: if God didn't listen to *his* prayer, maybe he would listen to others'. Prayer became something I depended on, and these four verses became nearest to my heart and mind.

ON MY KNEES

It's natural to want to keep those you love. Even though I knew being with Christ was better,[7] I didn't want my mother to be with him at that time. It's a likely guess that I was being common and selfish, possibly already experiencing parts of the grieving process. Months passed and almost every night before bed, my mom and I prayed.

I always prayed that God would remove the growth, but often the news received was that mom was stable. To me, stable, although better news than growth, was still disappointing and not good enough for me. There were times when the doctor reported shrinkage. It gave me hope, and I often told myself to pray harder believing Luke 18:1ff. Other times, news wasn't so good, and caused despair. It was an emotional roller coaster, but prayer was never compromised.

Overall, mom was doing well throughout the many months. Usually the report was that she was stable, good news. But, my soul was burdened and tears continued to flow.[8] I wanted a miracle. Not getting a miracle began to make my heart sick.[9] I needed the body of Christ to comfort me and offer hope.

WEANING FROM "ME" PRAYER TO "GOD" PRAYER

Prayer is a powerful tool, but the purpose and use of it is often misunderstood. Many of us most often come to prayer with a shopping list. Though supplication is a crucial aspect of prayer, it's not the only facet. At its core, prayer must have God-centric motive. A close relationship with God drives our prayer. Jesus teaches us to ask and it will be given to us.[10] And that if we ask in his name, it'll be done.[11] Scripture teaches us to ask. But prayer isn't just about asking. Jesus also teaches us to pray with God's will as our central request. Jesus prayed in Gethsemane asking his father to make a way to fulfill his mission without enduring or experiencing the cross. And, Jesus ended his prayer saying, "Your will be done."[12] If we go to God knowing he is sovereign, then we have peace that his will is best.

There are other conditions to having our prayers answered:

1. We can't regard wickedness in our heart.[13] The heart is the seat of our affections, the place of our preferences. God won't answer if wickedness has even remote fondness in my heart.

Praying with Mom

2. If my motives are wrong, or I desire my pleasure over God's.[14]
3. Belief must also be present, there's little room for doubt.[15]
4. In order to know and ask for God's will we must abide in Christ and get to know him through his word.[16]

A life of answered prayer isn't a life where we check off boxes in our shopping list. It's a life with God as first priority. We get to the point in our life where we desire his heart, his wants and his will more than our own. This is the core of intimacy. God reveals his heart and mind to those who walk intimately with him.

Mother often prayed for healing and believed God would do it, but she also realized that the will of God was beyond her comprehension. I wish I'd had a stronger prayer life before mom's illness. The times of prayer we shared together were sweet. I experienced that prayer makes our significant relationships more meaningful, and I began to love evenings praying with my mom.

She and prayer taught me a lot. Praying offered hope that God listens and heals. For mom it carried a sense peace that—regardless of the outcome—life and everything after would be ok. My love and appreciation for both mom and God grew. I learned that above all else, love satisfies. Praying with mom was one of the most satisfying things experienced throughout the diagnosis and illness. Regardless of the outcome, God gave cherished memories that are treasuries in my heart that'll reside there forever.

ENDNOTES

1. 1 Thess. 4:9–12.
2. Gal. 6:2.
3. The Bible often associates physical healing with demonic oppression and passages dealing with healing also deal with demon possession and casting out demons. In Greek, kai corresponds to the English conjunction *and*. Kai often is epexegetic which means that there exists a strong relation between the two words.
4. Gen. 25:21; Neh 1:6,11; Job 42:8–9; Psa. 102:17; Dan. 9:17–23; Matt. 21:22.

5. The church in Redding, CA is a member of the ministry HEALING ROOMS, http://healingrooms.com/. It was originally born out of the great Christian leader John G. Lake.
6. I believe it was Martin Luther.
7. Phil. 1:21–23.
8. Psalm 56:8.
9. Proverbs 13:12.
10. Matthew 7:7
11. John 14:13
12. Matthew 26:42.
13. Psalm 66:18.
14. James 4:3.
15. James 1:6–7.
16. 1 John 5:14–15; John 15:7.

6

Refreshment and Hope

May the Lord grant mercy to the household of Onesiphorus, for he often refreshed me.

—2 Timothy 1:16

Hope is patience with the lamp lit.

—Tertullian

One of the gloomiest novels written is *Frankenstein*. Unlike Hollywood, who associates the name Frankenstein with the monster, the book is about the creator and scientist, Victor Frankenstein. Written by Mary Shelley at a very young age, the story is told by an explorer named Robert Walton, who meets Victor Frankenstein in an area of the North Pole as the scientist searches for his monster to end his creation's existence.

Victor Frankenstein obsessed with creating life and applied all of his scientific knowledge to birthing a living being. After two years of hard work, Victor succeeded and the monster he so vigorously worked to create breathed life and greeted his maker with a grin. Surprisingly, after success and much hard work, Victor didn't respond with happiness over his achievement but revulsion at the gruesome, dreadful creature he brought into the world. This first rejection caused the monster great pain, which stoked a vengeful anger that drove the monster to kill Victor's brother.

The monster experienced rejection throughout the book by people in villages, families that he attached to and his creator, who is a father to him. Victor tried to create a mate for the monster but eventually stopped. The monster continued his rampage which climaxed with murdering Victor's wife. Without hope for reconciliation Frankenstein set out to find his creation and destroy it. In following clues, Victor is led to the North Pole where, on the brink of death, Robert Walton, the explorer that began and ended the book with letters to his sister, rescued him. In the end, Victor Frankenstein died and the monster came to mourn his creator, the only father he'd ever known. In the final segment of the novel the monster jumps from the cabin window of the ship as he tells Walton he's ending his life. The novel illustrates that without human connection, hope, and love the soul of a person dies. Even a created monster needs these to live.

Humankind has a similar plight. This world causes hearts to groan, spirits begin to choke when love, support and connection with others are absent. We need refreshment, encouragement and hope.

Hope is critical for vibrant Christian living. Without it, faith and love's full experience can't come to fruition. The soul can die a slow death without it.

Hearts become sick when burdened for a long period of time.[1] Though my mother was doing well as the months passed, God didn't answer my prayer for complete removal of the cancer growth. Because God wasn't totally removing my mother's cancer growth, a part of me was growing ill.[2] I still believed, but my soul wearied. It needed comfort.

UNEXPECTED HOPE FROM FRIENDS

A trip to England was necessary for my doctoral studies. My brother came to San Francisco to support mom while I was gone. Six months passed and mother was doing well, stable to slight shrinkage of the cancer. Still, the growth remained, and I continued deliberate prayer. The months of dealing with the situation wore me down. I needed hope. I needed comfort. I needed the body of Christ to minister to me.[3]

Praying with Mom

My heart was troubled leaving my mother for England, but she had good care in God's hands. I reminded myself that my responsibility was to do as much as I could, but ultimate responsibility was his.

Joseph Addison said, "When you say a situation or a person is hopeless, you are slamming the door in the face of God." As I look back on my first trip to the UK after mother's diagnosis, many brothers and sisters blessed me with encouragement and comfort during my stay. One particular friend was a man named Mick. Mick, a dear man that worked at the school for over twenty years could pass for Santa Claus if dressed in a red suit. Mick's prayer partner was a doctoral student in the UK, a godly, righteous man from Korea named Woosong. On one occasion, Mick was experiencing back pain and asked Woosong to pray for him. After Woosong's prayer, Mick's back healed. I asked Mick if he felt Woosong had the gift of healing.[4] Mick responded, "Yes." I immediately asked for Woosong's phone number and called his home. Woosong wasn't home, but his wife assured me that she'd pass the message to him. I looked forward to talking with him.

The next morning in the washroom I heard my name being called from the hallway. "Michael!" a man's voice shouted penetrating the washroom walls. "In a minute," I responded. When I exited the washroom, there was Woosong in the hallway. He looked like a sweet, peaceful angel sent from God, and that day he came with the assignment of offering me comfort and hope.

We went to my room, and I shared about mom's diagnosis—stage 4 lung cancer. Woosong told me stories of how he prayed for people with cancer, and how God often used prayer to bring about healing.[5] He told me of a British man with PSA that indicated severe cancer. After prayer, the PSA level measured at normal. PSA—for Prostate Specific Antigen—is a protein produced by cells of the prostate gland and is used as a tumor marker for prostate cancer.[6] He also told me about God, through prayer, causing tumors to shrink in two people with lung cancer.

Listening to Woosong's experiences brought great comfort. I was always skeptical about these types of stories in the past. Now the skepticism was engulfed by optimism.[7] The stories of God helping the sick brought me hope, encouragement and comfort. These people built me up, the very thing spiritual gifts in the body of Christ were meant for.[8] My spirit experienced peace, comfort and encouragement it hadn't encountered in a long time. My soul, a barren wasteland, began to breathe like fresh air after a heavy rain. God used Woosong to bring this encouragement.

We die without encouragement. The Bible is clear that encouragement is necessary to persevere in our faith.[9] The body of Christ is necessary to help those who are weak become stronger.[10] God used Woosong to fan life back into my weary heart. I felt refreshed, ready to live life with vitality.

Members of the body of Christ are crucial for growth, in maturing and enduring during devastation.[11] Woosong gave hope as well as challenge to my theological paradigms. I'd always believed gifts like healing ceased with the end of the Apostolic Age. But Woosong shared story after story about how God used prayers to bring about physical healing.[12] God uses people's gifts to bless and benefit others in the community of believers. First Corinthians 12:7 reads, "To each is given the manifestation of the Spirit for the common good." I certainly needed Woosong's gifts, and *that* day God used him for *my* good.

Later in the week Woosong had more good news to share with me. He said that while he and Mick were praying, Mick received a word from the Lord. He described it to me. The two were praying for my mother to be healed and Woosong felt impressed that my mother would be. This happened after Mick shared with Woosong his picture that came to him while he was praying. When Woosong shared this with me, my heart was overjoyed, and I had peace and happiness I'd not felt in months.

In the past, I never accepted interactions like this. Believing people received words from the Lord wasn't something suitable. Maybe I was so distraught in my soul that I was desperate for hope. Maybe the news of my mother's healing was too good to reject in the name of theological or doctrinal preferences. Despite my past skepticism, God used this prayer time between Mick and Woosong to lift my soul a bit more out of the mire.[13]

As I read the Scriptures, I found that "leading" by the spiritual realm wasn't uncommon.[14] I also couldn't find in Scripture where such gifts ceased.[15] In the past, I questioned people like Mick and Woosong, but now they became my teachers. I can't prove beyond a shadow of a doubt that the word from the Lord Mick received and Woosong's interpretation was 100 percent from God, but I confidently say God used it to infuse hope into my heart. Something I desperately needed.

Genuine hope is an inward quality that's a gift for the believer in Christ. The world can't offer hope like God can. When the world experiences suffering, God offers a better outcome and a deeper perspective. When our lives are in a valley, we cling to the truths of God's word that he turns valleys into gateways of hope. The temptation is to descend into despair or desolation. However, the valley welcomes a deeper level of intimacy with God that produces unique fruit that only germinates in desolation's soil. These valleys are part of the purposes of God to mature hope into a healthier condition. Without a maturing hope, the follower of Christ never fully experiences the joy of God's love and the blessing of holiness.[16]

The bitterness of life can be transformed into righteousness. Life's pain is a tool to lead us through God's gateway of genuine hope. The glory that will be revealed to us diminishes the suffering and pain this world throws our way.[17] Unlike Frankenstein and the monster he created, we must not despair.[18]

Mother and I continued to pray. Armed with new hope from friends as well as a new perspective on prayer, I proceeded to trust God for healing.

ENDNOTES

1. Jeremiah 8:18.
2. Proverbs. 13:12.
3. 1 Corinthians 12:7.
4. 1 Corinthains 12:29–30.
5. See Francis MacNutt *Power to Heal* (Notre Dame, Indiana: Ave Maria Press, 1977, 2001) for a good discussion from the perspective of someone who supports the healing gifts. From the perspective of suspicion and concern over those who are 'faith healers," see William Nolen M.D., *Healing: A Doctor In Search of a Miracle* (New York: Random House, 1974) where he chronicles his experience with the late faith healer Kathryn Kuhlman.
6. http://www.cancer.gov/cancertopics/factsheet/Detection/PSA
7. I need to briefly mention the issue of healing. I know there have been many abuses by the church within its history. Evangelists promise healing of a loved one if donations are given. People with certain belief systems declare a person healed and then healing never occurs.

Refreshment and Hope

If healing does not occur, some people's answer is, "You did not have enough faith." This statement is one of the most insensitive statements to make. The question arises, "What about your faith?" As if the person who prayed and claimed the healing is exonerated. Though there is biblical evidence that healing can be impeded by lack of faith, we cannot assume this is the case 100% of the time. The secret things belong to the Lord (Deut. 29:29).- Pedantic thinking and not very sensitive to hurting souls. - We must remind ourselves that our job is to offer our best. The rest is up to the Lord who can be fully trusted. Though my heart still hoped for a miracle, In time, I came to the conclusion that healing on earth was less relevant because for mom to be with Jesus was unfathomably better.

8. Ephesians 4:12–16.
9. Hebrews 10:25.
10. 1 Thessalonians 5:13–15; Romans 14:1–9.
11. The first person God used to bring me comfort was my good friend Greg Brown. We were already scheduled to meet and being with him the day after the news brought comfort to my heart.
12. There are many out there who do not hold to the 'sign gifts' like healing continuing on since Christ. On the issue of the sign gifts having ceased, see John MacArthur *Charismatic Chaos* (*Grand* Rapids: Zondervan, 1992). On the issue of sign gifts continuing, see Jack Deere *Surprised by the Power of the Spirit* (Grand Rapids: Zondervan, 1993). See also Wayne Grudem (ed.) *Are Miraculous Gifts for Today?* (Grand Rapids: Zondervan).
13. Psalm 40:2ff.
14. E.g., see Acts 20:23.
15. Some people can point to 1 Cor. 13:8–13. I am not defending a theological position that the sign gifts have ceased or not ceased. I have respect for both sides. The key issue is that God used the body of Christ to encourage me and refresh my soul.
16. Romans 5:4–5.
17. Romans 8:18.
18. 2 Coritnhains 4:8.

7

Darkness and Forgiveness

From within, out of the heart of man, come evil thoughts, sexual immorality, theft, murder, adultery, coveting, wickedness, deceit, sensuality, envy, slander, pride, foolishness. All these evil things come from within, and they defile a person.

—Mark 7:21–23

If you forgive the sins of anyone, they are forgiven;
if you withhold forgiveness from anyone, it is withheld.

—John 20:23

Everybody thinks of changing humanity,
but nobody thinks of changing himself.

—Leo Tolstoy

There's great evil in this world that causes great sadness. William Paul Young's book, *The Shack,* is the story about a father separated from God since his daughter's kidnapping and murder during a family camping trip. The main character, Mack, receives a note from God telling him to meet at the shack, the site of his daughter's brutal murder. Mack reluctantly accepts.

While at the shack, he encounters the Trinity and grows in his relationship and understanding of God.[1] Mack realizes God wasn't at fault for his daughter's death and juxtaposes to a new realization of who God is and how he works in the world. The Trinity gives assurance of God's love for he and his daughter, even obtains a glimpse of his daughter in paradise. This alone doesn't free Mack from his "great sadness." Only when he forgives his daughter's killer does he experience real freedom. Mack forces himself to say the words, "I forgive, I forgive, I forgive," and begins to let go of the hatred he has. The path of healing in his heart through internally forgiving over and over begins.

SEEING THE POOR HEALTH OF MY HEART

God showed me the sickness in my soul. I remember a speaker talking about a great saint of the church, George Mueller. Mueller, old and advanced in years, likely in his early nineties, was asked: "by now, your soul must be near perfection." Mueller's response: "The closer you get to the light, the more you see the spots." For me it wasn't close proximity to light but the darkness that revealed a lack of light and the presence of sin in my heart. C.S. Lewis once said, "The true Christian's nostril is to be continually attentive to the inner cesspool."[2] I didn't like the smell in mine.

ANOTHER CHALLENGE

It was already difficult to deal with the fact that mother had a severe diagnosis and could likely die soon. She also began to deal with emotional trauma. To make matters worse, a poorly handled misunderstanding between individuals led to mom and I being falsely accused.[3] I battled the hurt and grief of potentially losing my mother and now faced a new, unwanted challenge. I knew stress was the worst thing for mom's current health. She was more upset than I'd ever seen her. The issue had to do with money and an offended party feeling we were attempting to take it. The situation was totally blown out of proportion.

How could this happen at a time like this? I experienced first hand how unforgiving and malicious the heart can be. I desired to pray a Psalm of cursing for those causing so much strife.[4] An example from Psalm 11:5–6, "Let him rain coals on the wicked; fire and sulfur and a scorching wind shall be the portion of their cup." Another one from Psalm 35:8, "Let destruction come upon him when he does not know it! And let the net that he hid ensnare him; let him fall into it—to his destruction!" In my heart, I felt I had an enemy, and I wanted to pray an imprecatory Psalm upon the individuals.[5] I know in my heart that the Bible teaches forgiveness. Yet here the Bible offers an example to pray for an enemies' demise. Is this a contradiction? Is the Bible dependable and errorless?

I believe the great theologian John Calvin was correct when he described Psalms as theology of the heart. Psalms give us theological proxies and a glimpse into the human condition. Hurt attempts to work its bitterness into the human heart and soul. Throughout the Psalms reside cries of the heart—cries for deliverance; cries for help and for justice—that reflect the human heart as a wellspring of emotion. Nothing brings out negative emotions like an accuser.

I pondered long and hard to reconcile the requests for punishment in the Psalms with the New Testament teachings of forgiveness. The Bible was clear. John 20:23 says, "If you forgive the sins of anyone, they are forgiven; if you withhold forgiveness from anyone, it is withheld." I knew I couldn't stay in the Imprecatory Psalms.

CONTRADICTION?

Why does the Bible have Imprecatory Psalms while the New Testament clearly teaches forgiveness? I believe the Psalms of imprecation aren't meant to be an end but a means to an end—times in our life when pain is deep and we may not possess enough maturity to forgive immediately as Christ did.[6] So, the Psalms of imprecation bridge us into New Testament forgiveness. Praying these prayers acknowledges that a wrong occurs and justice is due. The plaintiff leaves the judgment of the accused in God's hands for justice, without taking it up ourselves. Once we acknowledge wrong and begin releasing justice into more capable hands, the Holy Spirit begins to heal and leads us to participate in forgiving. Still, it was hard to deal with my desire to pray a Psalm of Imprecation on my enemy, to see the darkness of my heart when wronged.

Darkness and Forgiveness

The Imprecatory Psalms were for me. My mom wasn't aware of them. Although forgiveness was a struggle for both of us, her heart was more forgiving. At night, she listened to sermons and shared with me minister's sermons on forgiveness. Stories of people with loved ones murdered who were later confronted by the murderer were common. In each case, God challenged hurt individuals to forgive. My mother told me she felt God leading her to forgive. All we were dealing with was a misunderstanding; others dealt with so much more.

WE ARE CAPABLE OF CHRIST-LIKENESS

Corrie ten Boom, a holocaust survivor helping Jews escape during World War II, faced one of the cruelest guards in her camp. At first reluctant to forgive him, she knew God's desire and asked God for strength to forgive. After forgiving the guard, Corrie ten Boom experienced more intensely God's love than ever in her life.[7] Martin Lloyd Jones once said, "Whenever I see myself before God and realize something of what my blessed Lord has done for me at Calvary, I am ready to forgive anybody anything. I cannot withhold it. I do not even want to withhold it."[8] The Bible is clear: we can't experience God's love without forgiveness. I knew in my heart I needed forgiveness and God's help to extend it.[9]

Almost everybody in the world experiences hurt from someone. If hurt remains without forgiveness then chaos ensues. Many of our world's troubles are rooted within a reluctance to forgive. Jesus' death is significant because the Bible reveals God's own pain, wrath and anger against sin.[10] Rather than condemning all of us to eternal punishment, God participates in redemptive forgiveness in Jesus Christ in order to quench his anger and remain a just God.[11] Christ absorbed our sin and the wrath of God on the cross.[12] We are never more a reflection of God than when we actively forgive.

AN OPPORTUNITY TO GLORIFY

Our human reaction when first hurt severely by another is to get even. Hatred, malice, and anger instinctively supersede love and forgiveness. During these times, much like Corrie ten Boom, we have opportunity to intensely experience God. Imprecatory Psalms can be used as steps to forgiveness. We pray the Psalms bridging us toward help and healing from our pain. We acknowledge wrong done to us and that God loves rightness and justice, but we can't remain there long. Our focus must turn back toward God, another common theme in Psalms.[13]

A GRACE DISGUISED

Next to the Bible, Jerry Sittser's book *A Grace Disguised*, had the most impact on me during the misunderstanding. Like Sittser, my life experienced loss, but unlike Sittser, my mother still lived.

Sittser's book leads through his journey of personal pain and suffering. One evening, returning home from an Indian reservation, a drunk driver strikes Sittser's vehicle. In a single event, Sittser loses his wife, mother and one of his children. In addition, his children that survive the crash are physically injured. It was all caused by a sole individual.

In one chapter Sittser describes dealing with the person who hit his car. Thoughts and desires of the person's demise often entered Sittser's thoughts. And, due to Sittser's lawyer's overconfidence and skillful arguments by the defense, the person who committed the crime was acquitted.[14] At this crossroad in his life one thing was clear, his life was septic.[15] Sittser writes:

> It eventually occurred to me that this preoccupation was poisoning me. It signaled that I wanted more than justice. I wanted revenge. I was beginning to harbor hatred in my heart. I was edging toward becoming an unforgiving person and using what appeared to be the failure of the judicial system to justify my unforgiveness. I wanted to punish the wrongdoer and get even. The very thought of forgiveness seemed abhorrent to me. I realized at that moment that I had to forgive. If not, I would be consumed by my own unforgiveness.[16]

Sittser goes on to say:

> The real problem . . . is not revenge itself but the unforgiving heart behind revenge. Unforgiveness is like fire that smolders in the belly, like smoke that smothers the soul. It is destructive because it is insidious. Occasionally it flares up in the form of bitter denunciation and explosions of rage. But most of the time it is content to stay low to the ground, where it goes unnoticed, quietly doing its deadly work.[17]

These words are the words of a prophet. My heart festered unforgiveness that warred against my soul.

The majority of what follows are excerpts from Sittser's book, his words still pierce my heart today. "Unforgiveness is . . . as ruinous as a plague. More destruction has been done from unforgiveness than all the wrongdoing in the world that created the conditions for it."[18] I had deep hurt against people falsely accusing mom and I. I struggled like Sittser. Sittser served as an example of forgiveness in the midst of deep loss and unfairness. He goes on to write:

> The process of forgiveness begins when victims realize that nothing—not justice or revenge or anything else—can reverse the wrong done . . . Victims can choose life instead of death . . . Forgiveness is simply choosing to do the right thing. It heals instead of hurts, restores broken relationships, and substitutes love where there was hate.[19]

The Asian culture has a streak of revenge in it. Growing up and watching Asian movies, revenge is a very common thread in the plot line. Human hearts naturally desire to get even, but Scripture clarifies that vengeance belongs to God.

Reading Sittser prompted me to see that my attitude and thoughts determine my heart, not my circumstances. "Forgiving people . . . simply let God be God so that they can be normal and happy human beings who learn to forgive. Rather than think that they must even all scores . . . and punish all wrongs, they simply choose to live as responsibly and humbly as they can."[20] Sittser also writes, "Forgiving people want God's mercy to win out. They want the world to be healed of its pain and delivered from the evil that threatens at every turn to destroy it utterly, including the evil that threatens to destroy their own souls."[21] These words guided me. My confused heart wanted vengeance but also deeply desired relief. The desire for revenge scorched my soul, and I needed the power of God to forgive. Just like Corrie Ten Boom and Jerry Sittser, God needed to heal me.

Sittser reminded me that it can be a process that may not happen instantaneously. He writes, "Forgiveness rarely happens in an instant . . . Forgiveness is more a process than an event, more a movement within the soul than an action on the surface, such as saying the words, 'I forgive you.'"[22] I began the journey of forgiveness.

Praying with Mom

LETTING GO, TRYING TO FORGIVE

One of the most powerful scenes in *The Shack* is when Mack must let go of his anger against the killer. God challenges him to say, "I forgive."[23] Although difficult, it definitely helps him take steps toward forgiving. The exercise proved helpful for me as I journeyed to forgive those hurting my mom and I. I often found myself reciting the phrase, "I forgive, I forgive, I forgive," much like Mack did in the novel.

Sittser goes on to write, "Though forgiveness may not have an ending, it has a beginning. It begins when victims identify the wrong done to them and feel the anger that naturally rises in the soul . . . Before they forgive, they must accuse."[24] Sittser then writes, "Forgiveness does not mean forgetting . . . In the end, I wonder whether it is really possible to forgive wrongdoers if we do not trust God first."[25] He closes the chapter by stating:

> "As I look back now, I see that no matter where I turned after my loss, I kept running into God. I shivered before the randomness of my suffering. I asked, "Why me?" I wrestled with unforgiveness. The questions I asked, the temptations I faced, the revenge I sought, the bewilderment I felt, and the grief I experienced all pushed me inexorably toward God."[26]

Indeed, forgiveness is more a journey that begins with a single act, a journey that can't be walked in one's own power, but in the power of our Lord. I learned that faith wasn't only necessary for physical healing in my mom's body, but also for spiritual healing in my own soul. The healing continues.

FORGIVENESS IN PEARL HARBOR

While visiting Pearl Harbor, I came across a sign about the leader of the first Japanese strike team leading the attack on Pearl Harbor, Mitsuo Fuchida. One phrase caught my attention, the sign read that Fuchida dedicated his life as a Christian minister after the war ended. I discovered a beautiful story of forgiveness and redemption from a little research.

Fuchida lived in post World War II Japan, a world of defeat. He came across a story about a prisoner of war named Jacob DeShazer.[27] The Doolittle Raid, America's response attack to Pearl Harbor, entrapped DeShazer. Filled with enough fuel to land in China, planes were sent to

Darkness and Forgiveness

strike Japan. DeShazer didn't reach China. He landed in Japan. This unfortunate event led to being a POW for almost 40 months—34 of those spent in solitary confinement. During his imprisonment, DeShazer was beaten, starved, and treated horribly. He witnessed the death of fellow POW's which fueled a growing bitterness and hatred toward the Japanese. Although he wasn't a Christian, while he was in jail he requested a Bible. He received one and began reading. Before leaving the Japanese prisons, he experienced the forgiveness of Christ.

Once released, DeShazer offered his life to serve God and enrolled in a Christian College. Three years later with his wife Florence, DeShazer returned to Japan, not for revenge, but to spend their years offering his life for the betterment of Japanese people. This, and other events like Luke 23:34 where Christ asks God to forgive the people judging and killing him, brought Fuchida to his knees. Fuchida saw in his heart the dark desire for revenge, but through the forgiveness of people like DeShazer, Fuchida gave his life to Christ. He served him the rest of his 26 years on earth. Had DeShazer not forgiven the people in Japan, we don't know how Fuchida's life might be different. Pearl Harbor was wrong, Fuchida admitted, and it wounded his soul. The wound coupled with the immense forgiving ability in God fueled Fuchida's life and ministry. He shared about God's redemptive forgiveness among the Japanese for the rest of his life. Those who forgive experience deep freedom—the freedom that I was seeking.

ENDNOTES

1. Paul Young, *The Shack* (Los Angeles, Windblown Media, 2007). There has been much controversy over this book. Some of advised against reading the book due to potential theological issues (e.g. the Trinity as a Black female (father), the Holy Spirit portrayed as an oriental woman). Others have felt that the book was a life changing experience. Given that the book is fiction and is based on how God healed Paul Young's pain, treating the book to much like a treatise would undermine its purpose: sharing how God changed a person thorugh a fictional tale..

2. See www.pietyhilldesign.com.

3. I apologize for being ambiguous at this point but in order to protect

individuals' identity, I must be vague with the facts. The issue had to do with money and a great misunderstanding became a horrible situation. One in which my mother was greatly insulted.

4. The Imprecatory Psalms were sections where the Psalmist desired a curse, judgment or misfortune on one or more persons.
5. Some Psalms where there are prayers of imprecation are 5, 6, 11, 12, 35, 37, 40, 52, 54, 56, 58, 69, 79, 83, 109,137, 139, and 143.
6. Luke 23:34.
7. See Corrie ten Boom, *Tramp for the Lord*, (Fort Washington, Pa., Christian Literature Crusade, 1974).
8. See pietyhilldesign.com.
9. John 15:7.
10. Romans 1:18–32.
11. Romans 3:23–25.
12. Colossians 1:19–23.
13. E.g. Psalm 13. My mother never prayed from the Imprecatory Psalms nor was aware that they existed.
14. Jerry Sittser *A Grace Disguised* (Grand Rapids: Zondervan, 2004, expanded edition) p.134.
15. Ibid. p.135.
16. Ibid. p.135.
17. Ibid. p.136.
18. Ibid. pp.136–137.
19. Ibid. p.141.
20. Ibid. p.143.
21. Ibid. p.144.
22. Ibid. p.144.
23. See Young, *The Shack*.
24. Sittser, *A Grace Disguised*, p.145.
25. Ibid. pp.146–147.

26. Ibid.p.147. Sittser also mentioned that dealing with the issue of forgiveness also lead him to ponder the sovereignty of God. The topic has already been dealt with in Chapter 4.

27. See also Jacob DeShazer as told to Don Falkenberg, *I was a Prisoner of Japan* (Tract). Columbus, Ohio: The Bible Meditation League, 1950.

8

Prayer, a Second Look

Rejoice always, pray without ceasing,
give thanks in all circumstances;
for this is the will of God in Christ Jesus for you.

—1 Thessalonians 5:16–18

And prayer is the turning away from ourselves to God in the confidence that he will provide the help we need. Prayer humbles us as needy, and exalts God as wealthy.

—John Piper

The apostle Paul always prayed for others, e.g., 1 Thess. 1:3. Prayer reveals the focus of our heart. Do we have a personal shopping list or are our prayers filled with pleading on behalf of others, e.g., 1 Thess.3:11–13? Prayer expresses our dependence on God. When we ask others to pray, we trust that their prayers help us. I needed all the help I could get, yet despite all of the good news, my prayers for healing went unanswered.

WHEN PRAYERS ARE NOT ANSWERED THE WAY WE PRAY

Despite having so many people around the world praying for my mom, she wasn't physically healed. She improved. Sometimes greatly, other times mildly, and sometimes she digressed. During this time of praying with mom, many people came into our lives that were also stricken with cancer. I promised to faithfully pray for them everyday. Many of them passed away, infusing in my heart an unwanted sadness. Young, old and middle aged, cancer didn't discriminate. The question that arose when faced with this reality was why? Why does our loving, all-powerful God not completely heal? Imagine the example to non-believers. Jesus healed throughout the Scriptures so that people witnessed his power as well as saw that he was indeed the living, Creator God. Why doesn't he do the same today? Isn't Jesus the same yesterday, today and forever?

I wish I could give a definitive answer to solve all of these questions, but faith believes with and without having answers. I'll give a shot at providing a semblance of an answer by acknowledging that the secret things belong to God.[2]

When our prayers' answers go against the way we hope, doubt comes. I prayed, and prayed, and prayed for a miraculous healing, it hadn't happened. Did I struggle with doubt? Yes. But, I realized that prayer is another means to experience God and not as a means to get what I want. The Bible teaches us that our purpose for prayer is to experience confidence that we're living the will of God.[3] To me, it seems obvious that miraculous healing should be the will of God.

Though I know and believe God does miraculously heal and do believe that our lack of faith can hinder it and cause God's inactivity,[4] I don't believe we can be dogmatic and assume that the automatic cause for God not answering a request exactly as we hope or ask is due to our lack of faith or sin. We accept that God's ways are higher than our ways. And, although it would make perfect sense for prayer to be answered a specific way, God doesn't always do what we ask and hope for. At this point, we trust in the character and perfection of God and acknowledge the aspects of supernatural mystery that accompany any journey of faith while we live and walk on this planet with an invisible God. Phillip Yancey writes:

> The only final solution to unanswered prayer is Paul's explanation to the Corinthians: "For now we see through a glass, darkly; but

then face to face: now I know in part; but then shall I know even also I am known." No human being, no matter how wise or how spiritual, can interpret the ways of God, explain why one miracle and not another, why apparent intervention here and not there. Along with the Apostle Paul, we can only wait and trust.[5]

There are many challenges we face that sometimes go unanswered: single people longing to be married that pray for a spouse; a loving parent prays for his/her child when they're ill; an unemployed father or single mom pray for a job with no success at finding work; someone diagnosed with bad health prays for healing; family members living in harmful ways are prayed for by believing family members. Prayer works, but results aren't the core purpose of prayer. They're only a means for us to test and see within our own heart. Sometimes we don't get what we pray for. The apostle Paul knew that in life after death his answered prayer resided, not in this present world.[6]

Are we entirely confident in God's character? All prayers *are* actually *answered*. God says yes, no or wait. Though my mother did well, God seemed not to grant my prayer for complete, miraculous healing. Prayer tests the depth of our belief and trust in God's goodness. The issue becomes, when we don't receive what we request or not in the way we hope for, do we still believe he's good? When he doesn't answer as quickly as we ask, does he still find faith and hope in me of his goodness?

Acts 12 records miraculous answer to prayer for imprisoned Peter. Acts 12:5 reads, "the church was earnestly praying to God for him."[7] Bound by chains, sleeping between two guards, and heavily guarded didn't prevent an angel from rescuing Peter. He goes to a friend's house. While they pray—to the surprise of many—Peter knocks on the door. One of numerous, miraculous answers to prayer that are recorded, something we all hope to experience.

The part of Acts 12 that we don't always mention is Acts 12:2. James the brother of John, apostle and son of Zebedee[8] dies by the sword, likely beheaded. The question becomes, did people pray for James? James was clearly imprisoned and free people were likely praying for him. Were prayers for Peter answered and prayers for James not?

Even during high points of God's Spirit moving among people, prayers were either unanswered or answered in a way seemingly contrary to the request. My guess? People were praying for James to be free just like they did Peter, but James didn't experience what Peter did. We might argue that James had a better plan from God, because in his death he experienced eternal life beyond earth earlier than Peter did.

When prayers go unanswered, or answered in a way contrary to the request we make, we must work through our doubt. When we come face to face with who God is and who we are, do we still trust, appreciate, and love him in the midst of it? Is God a cosmic Santa Claus? Is he there to fulfill my desires? And, who am I? Am I the center of the universe or is God? Job didn't get answers from God, he got God. Is that who I find at the end of my prayers? I must remind myself what the purpose of prayer is: not to get what I want, but to get what I most desperately need, God.

I prayed and prayed for healing and asked men and women all over the world to pray for mom. I heard mom talk on the phone with her friends always happy to share with people all around the world that were praying for her. People prayed in the UK, US, Canada, Honduras, Iran, Korea, China, Tanzania, Ghana—to name a few. Yet, despite effort, care and faith from people around the world praying, mom didn't completely heal the way we asked him. It tested me to see if I truly believed. It tested my motives for prayer: was it for me or was it to discover and encounter God at the end of them?

ENDNOTES

1. Hebrews 13:8.
2. Deuteronomy 29:29.
3. 1 John 5:14–15.
4. 1 Corinthians 11:23–30.
5. Phillip Yancey, *Prayer: Does It Make a Difference?* (Grand Rapids: Zondervan, 2006), 247.
6. Romans 8:18–28; Philippians 1:19–24.
7. TNIV
8. Matthew 4:21.

9

Pride

A man's pride brings him low, but a man of lowly spirit gains honor..
—PROVERBS 29:23

God sends no one away empty except those who are full of themselves.
—DWIGHT L. MOODY

CHARLES DICKENS IS CONSIDERED one of Britain's greatest novelists. He started out poor but ended life as a successful writer. The eighth novel from his pen, *David Copperfield,* is about an adult reflecting on life from childhood to the present. *David Copperfield* parallels Dickens' own life, and many literary scholars hold the book as autobiographical.

One of the book's main themes criticizes the value society places on individuals based on wealth and status. It doesn't conclude that *all* rich people are arrogant. There are characters in the book that are well off while not being haughty to the poor and poorer characters that cheat. But Dickens spends a great deal of the writing condemning affluence and class as determining factors for measuring a person's worth. He challenges his readers not to look at their status to determine their value but to check their inner character and service to society. Pride becomes an important theme. The great English Puritan, Richard Baxter, lamented on pride: "Oh what a constant companion, what a tyrannical commander, what a sly and subtle insinuating enemy, is this sin of pride!"[1]

Pride

This attitude of superfluous superiority surfaced in my own heart. God revealed to me my conceit toward people of other faiths and how my ignorance grew into pride. Slowly, I recognized the ways that I too, like characters in Dickens' book, looked down on certain denominations and groups of people based on the fact that I felt I had greater understanding and practice in Scripture. God showed me the wonderful beauty and love that exists in the heart of many who love and serve the Lord. Edward Payson describes pride well. "Pride consists in an unduly exalted opinion of one's self. It is, therefore, impatient of a rival, hates a superior, and cannot endure a master."[2]

Unbelief and pride are best friends. Where one is, the other isn't far behind. I'm convinced that those who want to draw close to our Lord must have the pride that's in their hearts and souls pressed out of them.

Humility can be a choice. Take Hezekiah's example in 2 Chronicles 32:26, "Hezekiah humbled himself for the pride of his heart, both he and the inhabitants of Jerusalem, so that the wrath of the LORD didn't come upon them in the days of Hezekiah." God hates pride, "The fear of the LORD is hatred of evil. Pride and arrogance and the way of evil and perverted speech I hate." (Prov. 8:13) We do have a choice. Humankind can chose humility. I needed to learn the hard way.

My haughty attitude puffed up toward many groups: Charismatic/Pentecostal, Catholic, and another group that I'll write about later. I have disagreements with some views within these groups, but I now realize that my disagreements were deeper. I felt higher than them. God taught me that he has those who love Him in many places that might surprise us. I found very dedicated people within various groups of believers that God used to help me. It caused me to rethink my paradigms.

I still have disagreements with certain practices and beliefs, but at the heart of the issue for me was whether or not a person believes and is a part of the family of Christ. My answer to these groups of people that I once disdained was: not all of those in these groups were apostate. There were believers among them that I'll see in heaven. At the heart of the matter remains, is God's law written in their heart. Jeremiah 31:33–34 says:

> "But this is the covenant that I will make with the house of Israel after those days, declares the LORD: I will put my law within them, and I will write it on their hearts. And I will be their God, and they shall be my people. And no longer shall each one teach his neighbor and each his brother, saying, 'Know the LORD,' for they

> shall all know me, from the least of them to the greatest, declares the LORD. For I will forgive their iniquity, and I will remember their sin no more."

Did God write his law on their hearts? Are there members in these groups that are my brothers and sisters? The answer to these questions for me was yes and that the root of the problem was pride. God showed me that the varieties of people that glorify his name are diverse. Almost every church leaning more toward the Pentecostal/Charismatic faith saw people healed. I found healing in many Catholic groups as well. Yet for me, seeing people healed wasn't common in my faith growing up. Many lives among these groups of people that I'd disdained taught me. Why was God using them? After much thought, I concluded that they had a simple faith and believed God (James 1:6–8).

JAMES 5:14-15

Simple faith means believing God's word. Faith and the word of God are linked (Rom. 10:17-21). We must take God at his word and live it out to have real, experiential faith. James 5:14-15 straightforwardly says, "Is anyone among you sick? Let him call for the elders of the church, and let them pray over him, anointing him with oil in the name of the Lord. And the prayer of faith will save the one who is sick, and the Lord will raise him up." Very clear and concise, yet I had doubts. If God is sovereign then why do I need to call the elders of the church to pray and anoint with oil? Is prayer not enough? I later called a friend whose wife was miraculously healed of back cancer, and I asked him if he asked the elders of the church to pray and anoint her with oil. His answer was profound, "Yes, that's what the Bible says to do." I had to call on someone who had already seen cancer healed to teach me that I could trust the reliability of the Bible and that I wasn't wasting my time phoning the church to ask the elders to pray.

Mother and I were attending a church at the time called Central Peninsula Church in the Bay area. I called the church office on Monday to ask them if they prayed for the sick and anointed with oil. The person at the church said they did and immediately transferred me to the pastor's office. I left a message for the pastor on his voicemail and later found out that he attended to my message even though it was his day off. I know he didn't need to do it and likely needed the rest, but I really appreciated his effort. That Sunday, between services, the elders and the pastor gathered in his office and prayed for my mother, anointing her with oil. After they finished praying and anointing, my mom said, "The cancer is gone." I think it was more her expressing appreciation and gratitude for their service as she was very thankful for the pastor and elders to take time, but I also believe the Spirit spoke through her. The Spirit spoke to me, and I realized my faith was small.

I would much rather possess humility than pride. Pride prevents us from believing God for who he is and believing God's infallible Word because we're blinded by ourselves. Not just exaggerating our own importance, but also our fears and insecurities that let pride act as a defense mechanism. God slowly removed my defense mechanisms, but he was far from finished.

MY ATTITUDE

God continued to show me *how* prideful I was. He already revealed some attitudes toward different denominations. I thought in my mind that I'd worked through most of them, but I had another bias, I didn't like the Amish. In my mind they were always a secretive culture that I judged a bit cultic; they were evil. My belief later shifted.

October 2, 2006, Charles Carl Roberts entered an Amish schoolhouse at approximately 10:25 am EDT. Five girls died, and the others sent into critical care. My first thought was that the Amish were being punished for their sin. I couldn't have been farther from the truth. Here's an excerpt that summarizes the situation well:

> The gunman, Charles Carl Roberts, backed a pickup truck up to the front of the Amish schoolhouse and entered the school at approximately 10:25 am EDT, shortly after the children had returned from recess. He allegedly asked the teacher, Emma Mae Zook, and the students if they had seen a clevis pin missing along the road. Survivors later recounted that Roberts was mumbling his words and was not making direct eye contact with anyone. After the occupants of the classroom denied seeing any such object, Roberts walked out to his truck and reappeared in the classroom holding a 9mm handgun. He ordered the male students to help him carry items into the classroom from the back of his pickup. Zook and her mother, who was visiting the schoolhouse, took this oppor-

tunity to escape the school and ran towards a nearby farm to get help. Roberts saw the people leave, and ordered one of the boys to stop them, threatening to shoot everyone if the women got away. Still, Zook and her mother managed to reach the farm, where they asked Amos Smoker to call 911 . . . At approximately 11:07 am Roberts began shooting the victims. As the first trooper in line reached a window, the shooting abruptly stopped. Roberts had committed suicide.

It took the troopers about two and a half minutes to break into the school to assist those children who were not killed instantly. Reports stated that most of the girls were shot "execution-style" in the back of the head. The ages of the victims ranged from six to thirteen.[3]

AMISH RESPOND WITH FORGIVENESS

It was a shocking national event that ultimately changed my life. The Amish responded with such an incomprehensible example of supernatural love and modeled to me the love of Christ in a way that I knew I couldn't have responded had I experienced anything similar. God showed me how much hurt was in my heart and how little love resided there. After I saw the Amish respond I knelt down and asked God to forgive me of my judgmental sin toward Amish people. Only people who loved Christ could respond with such supernatural love and forgiveness. Here's another excerpt of their example:

> On the day of the shooting, a grandfather of one of the murdered Amish girls was heard warning some young relatives not to hate the killer, saying, "We must not think evil of this man." Another Amish father noted, "He had a mother and a wife and a soul and now he's standing before a just God."
>
> Jack Meyer, a member of the Brethren community living near the Amish in Lancaster County, explained: "I don't think there's anybody here that wants to do anything but forgive and not only reach out to those who have suffered a loss in that way but to reach out to the family of the man who committed these acts."
>
> A Roberts family spokesman said an Amish neighbor comforted the Roberts family hours after the shooting and extended forgiveness to them. Amish community members visited and comforted Roberts' widow, parents, and parents-in-law. One Amish man held Roberts' sobbing father in his arms, reportedly for as long

as an hour, to comfort him. The Amish have also set up a charitable fund for the family of the shooter. About 30 members of the Amish community attended Roberts' funeral, and Marie Roberts, the widow of the killer, was one of the few outsiders invited to the funeral of one of the victims. Marie Roberts wrote an open letter to her Amish neighbors thanking them for their forgiveness, grace and mercy.

She wrote, "Your love for our family has helped to provide the healing we so desperately need. Gifts you've given have touched our hearts in a way no words can describe. Your compassion has reached beyond our family, beyond our community, and is changing our world, and for this we sincerely thank you." [4]

RESPONDING TO THE DANGEROUS WORLD WE LIVE IN

One reason why life is difficult is because people are capable of evil. From a haughty heart to mass murder, there's evil in our flesh (Romans 7:20). That's the world we live in. Read or turn on the evening news and every day tragic events throughout our world get reported, often crimes against our own humanity. Within circles of friends bad news occurs: a friend gets a terminal diagnosis; a spouse cheats after years of marriage; a loved one suddenly passes; a child is shot; people swindled of their money. We live in a world where bad things happen. We're all subject to the hurt and cruelty of the world. The Amish experienced it first hand and responded in a way that reflected Christ.

In a world of cruelty and hate, the best solutions call us to respond with the Spirit of Christ. I wouldn't have been able to respond the way the Amish did. When people treated my mother and I poorly, my heart angered, hated and wanted to avenge, but the Amish didn't respond that way. When I read accounts of their forgiveness for the family and inviting the widow to the funeral, I realized that I fell far short of Christ.[5] The Amish people showed their love for the Lord. Their response to brutality in this world should be emulated by all of us who ask God to forgive us by believing Christ is Lord. The behavior of Amish people revealed pride in my heart. I had limited knowledge and interactive experience with them and had unfairly chosen to prematurely judge them. The gift they gave through their living what they believe continued to teach me.

ENDNOTES

1. http://www.pietyhilldesign.com/gcq/quotepages/pride.html
2. www.pietyhilldesign.com
3. Taken from http://en.wikipedia.org/wiki/Amish_school_shooting
4. Ibid.
5. 1 Corinthians 11:1.

10

Insecurity

Such is the confidence that we have through Christ toward God. Not that we are sufficient in ourselves to claim anything as coming from us, but our sufficiency is from God.

—2 Corinthians 3:4–5

In a world we find terrifying, we ratify that which doesn't threaten us.
—David Mamet

Insecurity is a disease that plagues humanity. It's an enemy to all those who desire a surrendered life to God. Insecurity enslaves, thrusting the responsibility of our protection on possessions, activities, and ourselves.

Literature is filled with characters plagued by this disease. In Arthur Miller's *Death of a Salesman*, Willy Loman is the main character working at the same company for over thirty years. Willy has a strong desire to be recognized and adored by people and a particular desire for the love and affection of his son. Because of these issues, Willy lies, fearing that if people really know who he is they won't accept him. He lives in a world of delusion and denial. Willy is surrounded by those who are more successful: his neighbor, his deceased brother—which Willy idolizes, his boss—who is younger, and his neighbor's son—a successful lawyer. These characters represent all that Willy isn't. Rather than accepting who he is and trying to make things better, Willy lies to his family and to himself, and in the end, he takes his life. It's a grim tale of a man destroyed by his own insecurity without the courage to face the truth, accept who he is, and conquer the need to be something he's not. All of humanity faces the same challenges to overcome as Willy Loman.

Entire cultures express this need for security. India has a caste system. Europe has monarchies. And capitalist countries have economic classes that determine the "pecking order" of social respect. The wealthier, more socially successful or refined are at the top, while those who are poorer and less desirable are at the bottom. In all levels of education, there are popular kids and those kids that don't quite fit in. In workplaces people gain respect by climbing the corporate ladder, producing desired results and profits. In sports the player who makes the winning score or winning save gets glory, while those who give up the winning points become scapegoats. Stardom and shame are separated by the thinnest of lines. The world's cultures easily believe that more is better and people need to achieve in order to gain significance.

These attitudes contradict Scripture. Humankind's worth lies in being "fearfully and wonderfully made. Wonderful are your works; my soul knows it very well."[1] Our value isn't due to achievement. The way up in Christ isn't to ascend to the highest position but to become a servant.[2]

PRIDE REVEALS INSECURITY

The pride God showed me toward the Amish also revealed an insecure heart. I wanted people to love me. I wanted my mom to be an example to everyone of how a person goes about getting someone healed. I trusted in my own ability and success, not the Lord's. It wasn't a fun or easy time but a time when God rooted out hurts and pains that were causing my soul not to rest in him. I read books on healing and began to place my trust in my own effort to pray right and have faith rather than in the security of sovereign God.

Another hard aspect for me was to see people I'd gone to school with and fellow classmates moving up in their careers. I had friends becoming country directors where they were responsible for people of an entire country. I saw friends becoming area directors responsible for work in many countries. I had friends starting schools in faraway places, friends

Insecurity

teaching at prestigious schools, friends making big salaries at prominent companies. It seemed like everyone else moved on and up while I remained idle. Over time it bred in me a sense of insignificance and inferiority. After regrouping and realigning my thought life, I realized that my task was also important. I was reminded these things don't impress God like they do humanity. Humility and reverence toward his word impresses God.[3]

After refocusing and reorienting I quickly realized that the assignment my mom and I had was the most important undertaking in my life. I knew that a lifetime of happiness and guilt would be influenced by how I valued these moments with mom. If I turned my back on her to pursue my own interests, a lifetime of regret would follow with only an unsatisfying sense of false achievement to overcompensate. I knew that time with my mother, however long or short, was every bit as significant as the greatest accomplishment through any interests I'd pursued in life so far.

During this period, a prominent pastor called and asked me to consider helping as he established another ministry. Although the observation that friends had already accomplished great things compelled me, I knew the opportunity had to be put on hold. The relationship and health of mom became the priority of my life.

INSECURITIES' OFFSPRING

Insecurity breeds evil descendants much like fear. The Bible clearly encourages believers to not be afraid.[4] The commands, "do not be afraid" or "do not fear" are possibly the most often mentioned commands in the Bible. A search on the phrase "do not be afraid/do not fear" yields references throughout both the Old and New Testaments.[5] Why does the Bible denounce fear so much? Fear wars against faith. Godly fear is to "fear God."[6] Fear in anything other than God leads our journey to unbelief. Whether the threat is authentic or imagined, fear causes us distress. Always feeling threatened reveals our need to hope in the Lord.[7] Godly fear leads to reverential awe of God. When fear outside of God engulfs us, it's a sign of potential disrespect toward God. Insecurity breeds *this* type of fear.

The fear of losing my mom was strong, I didn't want to live a life without her. The fear of losing her too soon was a challenge to my faith.

Would I continue to believe that God was powerful and good if he took her away? Could I trust God if he chose not to heal her? Would I believe he still held the best plans for life? These challenged my faith as I wrestled with the fear of losing a loved one.

Another evil descendant that insecurity breeds is doubt. Doubt leads to lack of assurance. Living life with a lack of assurance is a bumpy, unpeaceful life. Christ assures believers that one day he'll return and make all things new.[8] This assurance doesn't need delay until Christ's return, the experience begins now.[9] Christ's return drove Paul.[10] He desired his converts to have this mindset of Christ's return as a hope that compelled their lives.[11]

I needed assurance as doubt, fear and insecurity attacked my faith. Seeing mom go in for treatment chipped away at my heart as she repeatedly lay down while chemotherapy pumped into her body. Why would a good and powerful God allow this? Why didn't he just heal her? Why did he allow mom and I to suffer like this? So many issues wrestled with my heart.

Insecurity breeds anxiety. Anxiety makes the mind uneasy, fearful of things that often never happen. Peace rips away at the heart and soul. Psychiatry understands anxiety as a mental disorder of unusual apprehension and psychic strain. Anxiety robs the peace that God brings.

WARFARE WEAPONS AGAINST INSECURITY

We fight insecurity and its many offspring—fear, doubt, anxiety—with the weapons of prayer, thankfulness, and faith.[12] We engage our mind with what's true, honorable, just, pure, lovely, commendable, excellent, praise worthy.[13] God's peace crushes insecurity's leading and its brood.

Only a life centered on God discovers lasting security. An insecure life easily blows with the world's gushing hard winds. When Job suffered tragedy after tragedy he responded steadfast to his God. Job 1:20-22, "Then Job arose and tore his robe and shaved his head and fell on the ground and worshiped. He said, "Naked I came from my mother's womb, and naked shall I return. The LORD gave, and the LORD has taken away; blessed be the name of the LORD." In all of this Job didn't sin or charge

God with wrong. When life's winds try to dislodge us with our insecurities, we must respond in worship like Job: "Blessed be the name of the Lord."

Cain was very insecure.[14] Rather than facing the fact that he wasn't as devoted as his brother Abel, Cain went sins' way and attempted to eliminate what he thought was his source of distress. Cain wasn't an atheist; in fact, he had clear communication with God. Yet it wasn't enough to offset the wickedness within his human heart. Insecurity often leads to riddance rather than repentance.

Humankind frequently wants proof of the glory of God by signs and wonders, but the Old Testament proves that the physical presence of God isn't enough. Humankind consistently still chooses evil over obedience. Cain slew his brother despite the physical presence of God being so strong during that period of time in history. Israel had the physical presence of God by day in the form of a cloud, and the physical presence of God by night in the form of a ball of fire. When it moved, the nation moved. Was that enough? Despite daily offerings by the Priests and Levites, the nation chose sin over obedience.[15] God's physical presence didn't quench the sinful human condition and tendencies.

In the story of Lazarus and the rich man both passed and went to Abraham's bosom. The rich man requested to go back and warn his family. Yet Abraham told him that they have the Law and the Prophets, if they didn't listen to them, they certainly wouldn't listen to a dead man's warnings.[16]

The Pharisees and Sadducees demanded a sign from Jesus;[17] our Lord didn't give them one and condemned their faith as wicked. Jesus referenced that he'd die and rise from the dead as the sign.

We overestimate the impact of wonders. Although God uses wonders to prove his presence and power, signs and wonders shouldn't be primary anchoring for our belief in God. Even when God chooses not to do the extraordinary, we still need to believe. I needed to accept this fact if I wanted peace in my soul.

More examples of people's insecurity include: Saul trying to eliminate David, Herod trying to eliminate Jesus. Each has a common thread. When personal security is threatened, sin's way is to seek removal. God's way is repentance and worship. Had Cain repented and worshipped, had Saul repented and worshipped, had Herod repented and worshipped, the Bible would record very different outcomes to their lives.

Philemon experienced a challenge to his security. His slave, Onesimus, escaped from his service. Under Roman law, this carried a death penalty. Paul appeals to his fellow believer for the safe return and reinstatement of Onesimus. He requests that he not only be reinstated but elevated to a position above slave/servant—beloved brother. Scripture doesn't give us the rest of the story. It leaves us to guess and speculate. Holy Scripture likely wouldn't have included this story had Onesimus's fate been one of punishment and wrath instead of love and grace. Philemon confronted a difficult circumstance and likely didn't choose the way of the world, or the ways of our natural inclination, but of grace. *That's how to deal with insecurity.*

For me, seeing my mother's healing was important. I pleaded to God on behalf of her gifting. Mother was a gifted speaker and writer who was already being used, why not use her more? Why not use her to reach Mandarin Chinese speaking people with the Gospel? Much of my security rested in the hope of mom's healing rather than the hope of God's sovereignty. Like Philemon, the challenge to my security offered me a dose of humility. How would I take it?

ENDNOTES

1. Psalm 139:14.
2. Mark 10:45.
3. Isaiah 66:1–2.
4. E.g. Luke 8:50.
5. E.g. Gen 43:23; 46:3; Deu.1:9; Josh.1:9; 10:25; 11:6; Psa. 56:4; Jer. 1:8; Matt. 14:27; Acts 27:24; Rom. 13:4; Rev. 2:10.
6. Psalm 67:7; 111:10; Ecc. 12:13.
7. Psalm 45:2.
8. Rev. 21.
9. Psalm 67:7; 111:10; Ecc. 12:13.
10. Phil. 1:6, 10.
11. 1 Thess. 5:8.
12. Phil. 4:6–7.

13. Phil 4:8.
14. See Genesis 4.
15. Of the five books of the Pentateuch, the book of Numbers offers the best picture of this.
16. See Luke 16:19–31.
17. Matthew 16:1–4

11

Finding Love

House and wealth are inherited from fathers, but a prudent wife is from the LORD.

—Proverbs 19:14

No one warns young people to follow Adam's example. He waited till God saw his need. Then God made Adam sleep, prepared for his mate, and brought her to him. We need more of this 'being asleep' in the will of God. Then we can receive what He brings us in His own time, if at all. Instead we are set as blood-hounds after a partner, considering everyone we see until our minds are so concerned with the sex problem that we can talk of nothing else when bull-session time comes around. It is true that a fellow cannot ignore women---but he can think of them as he ought---as sisters, not as sparring partners.

—Jim Elliot (written while single)

One of the greatest pieces of romantic literature is Shakespeare's *Romeo and Juliet*. The one important theme? Love's power. This love isn't the silly, childish portrayal often depicted in television and romantic Hollywood films, but one filled with deep emotion, undying commitment, endurance through affliction and ultimately death.

Finding Love

Despite institutional and familial pressures, Romeo and Juliet fought for their love. The feuding of the two families produced an environment ill-suited for marriage, so Romeo and Juliet conducted their relationship in private. In the end a failed plot by Friar Laurence led to the two young lovers uniting in death, bringing peace to the feuding families as they saw the tragedy in their foolishness and the pride that caused the most cataclysmic of occurrences. In the end, love conquered and proved to be the only power able to produce peace in war. Shakespeare illustrated that without love, people die, and death is better than being unloved. Consequently, humankind naturally seeks love.

Holy Scripture is a love story about a loving God allowing his creation to freely choose him. The rest of history is God wooing his creation back into relationship through his sending his son to die for it. No greater love exists than to lay down our own life for another. God is love, and he actively demonstrates it throughout history and the Bible.

No book expresses God's romantic side towards his people quite like Hosea. God has the anger of a betrayed spouse and commanded his prophet Hosea to marry a prostitute named Gomer. God was hurt by Israel's departure and compared it to being married to a whore. But God didn't let his anger seethe. He continued to woo his people. Hosea 2:14–16 says:

> Therefore I am now going to allure her; I will lead her into the desert and speak tenderly to her. There I will give her back her vineyards, and will make the Valley of Achor a door of hope. There she will sing as in the days of her youth, as in the day she came up out of Egypt. "In that day," declares the LORD, "you will call me 'my husband'; you will no longer call me 'my master.'

Our God, who could easily have his creation vanquished, continues to lovingly woo his people into communion with himself.

PRAYERS FOR A MATE

For almost forty years, I battled singleness. Though my quest for love was nowhere near as challenging as that depicted by Shakespeare, the power and passion of it were true in my heart. Although I had much love from friends and family, I desired the love of a mate. I believed that if God never provided a wife for me, I'd be happy and content, yet a longing in my heart remained.

Singleness can be a struggle. Loneliness is one of the hardest emotions to deal with. The pain of emptiness magnifies in circumstantial solitude. I remember desiring a mate and praying for one at eighteen years old. I also remember how hard it was to be single, desiring a mate. Seeing people all around dating and falling in love while I wasn't in a significant relationship was difficult. Watching friends marry while I didn't even have dates didn't help.

Asking women out on a date can terrify men. Rejection is as painful as loneliness, and putting ourselves on the line to be rejected can form some painful moments and memories. A young lady accepting my request for a date brought joy, but, on the flip side, a decline caused disappointment.

Loneliness is part of life. People from all stages, not just the unmarried, experience it. Spouses lose each other through divorce or death. Married couples experience loneliness through infertility, consistently coming up short conceiving, close friends moving away, a parent or loved one dying, marriage becoming stale and routine, a friend's unexpected unavailability, someone not loving you back or loving someone else, people ignoring us when we're in a group, classmates making fun because we're not cool enough or don't quite fit in. Loneliness takes many forms.

God often called people when they were in solitude. Christianity is community, but the callings within Christianity are often individual.[1] God called Abraham alone.[2] The result of the call: a twenty-five year journey waiting for the instruction to reach completion.

Was Abraham anxious? Did he doubt? Genesis 16 seems to answer yes. Eleven years is a long time to wait, and I'm guessing Abraham and Sarah were tormented with impatience coupled with doubt. As a result, the birth of Ishmael via Hagar with its effects still felt today.[3] Fourteen years after the birth of Ishmael, God fulfilled his promise. Isaac was born.

But in Genesis 22, God calls Abraham to sacrifice Isaac. Abraham waited about twenty-five years for this son from Sarah to arrive, and now God asks something seemingly irrational? Abraham appears to obey without flinching. He doesn't question God like he did when God revealed to him his plan to destroy Sodom and Gomorrah—Abraham's nephew happened live there. Abraham simply appears to pack up and prepare for the three day journey with his son.

I believe the longest and loneliest part of Abraham's journey wasn't the twenty-five years waiting for Isaac to be born but possibly the three day journey he took with his son to Mount Moriah.[4] During those three days to Mount Moriah, I imagine Abraham looking at his son with thanksgiving and heartfelt smiles. Scripture says Abraham knew and believed God would raise his son from the dead.[5] The three day journey gave Abraham time to reflect on his twenty-five years of waiting as well as the time that remained for him with his son.

Sometimes it seems God is doing something contrary to his promises. If he's good, then why do I feel so bad? If he's all I need, then why this strong desire for something else? It's clear that humankind isn't meant to be alone. Even though Adam wasn't corrupted by sin, even though he had meaningful work, even though he had a direct relationship with God, it was still, "not good for him to be alone."[6] God created a helpmate for him.

PATIENTLY WAITING

We enjoy relationships, and marriage is one of the most desperately sought. It was a deep longing for me. Even though I had a growing relationship with the Lord and my mother was ill, I still desired to marry. At night, mom and I prayed. Sensing her time could be short, mom prayed for a mate for me. I echoed the prayers and also prayed that mom would meet her and get to know her.

A mother's love can be one of the purest in the universe. Mothers who experience dire circumstances are often still inclined to serve children before their own personal needs and wants. Even though mom was diagnosed with a terminal disease, she desired to see her son taken care of.[7]

Life's circumstances can be hard, and it's easy to be like Abraham and Sarah in Genesis 16. Some people forfeit God's bountiful blessing because they don't trust enough to endure seasons of solitude. Others come to grips with their circumstances and accept the situation as a blessing. For me, waiting for a mate seemed like a long journey, one that began at age eighteen—likely even younger. Although I desired marriage, I didn't seek it out much. My mother was the priority of my life, her needs were more important than mine.

SEEING THE ANSWER

Mom wanted to visit China in order to revisit the home where she grew up. My brother accompanied her. While she was on the trip, I returned to Ohio. I wanted to take a trip to visit a professor from Seminary. Having relocated to teach at Gordon-Conwell Theological Seminary in South Hamilton, Massachusetts, he was no longer at my old school. I realized my perspective on life had changed, time on earth was limited. I had to make decisions in life based on a new perspective.

Time with those we love and care for is our most valuable asset and greatest commodity. Often, our focus is on productivity instead of relationships, getting things done instead of sipping coffee with a friend. I asked myself whether or not I'd regret not trying to visit my professor if the Lord were to take him. My answer was yes, so I quickly emailed his wife. She replied back and told me they were free at the time of my break. I scheduled the road trip from Ohio to Boston.

It was a refreshing and blessed time in the New England area. Wonderful fellowship and beautiful scenery, Boston has always been a special place for me. Something about New England refreshes my soul. Spending time with my Professor and his wife revived and refreshed my heart too, like fresh rain on a barren, dry dessert. Without love, we die.

THE PERFECT PLAN

One day while visiting, my Professor's wife returned from shopping with a friend. Her first words to me were, "Have I got a plan for your life." I thought she found a ministry for me to serve in or a church to pastor. I was way off. She was thinking romance.

While shopping for groceries with a friend, an idea came to both of them. There was a young, attractive, godly young woman visiting at the seminary, and both women knew her. Before either could muster up words they both knew from the look in each other's eyes what the other was thinking. Match making was their plan for the day.

They told me their idea. My professor's wife and friend seemed very excited about the potential match. After being interviewed by her friend, both felt connection would benefit. I agreed to it, but I had one condition. I needed a picture. Providentially, pictures were available to view. After seeing pictures, I supported the meeting.

Finding Love

FIRST DATE

The brisk New England morning had dew on the ground and fresh air to breathe, sunny, clear skies and comfortable temperatures with a perfect fall day forecast. Breakfast cooked in my Professor's apartment filling it with the smell of eggs and coffee. Coffee and breakfast weren't the only things filling my head.

As I sat on the couch waiting to meet "the girl"—named Jodi—I was concerned about how we'd interact, the pictures attracted me but would we have chemistry when we met? Upon my request, I asked those that "set us up" not to divulge the set-up. My thinking was it might make her uneasy and anxious and prevent us from natural interaction. The logic behind my reasoning was less pressure, more comfort.

Jodi arrived at the apartment with a friend. I rose and introduced myself. It was a casual breakfast around a table filled with old and new friends. Jodi wasn't fooled and knew it wasn't a random occurrence. Friends' intentions were obvious as people made excuses to leave the room while we remained together. Alone. While doing the dishes, Jodi and I had time to interact.

It was easy to be around her. Later, we decided to go to a nearby town named Rockport. Throughout the day, I felt I was with someone I'd known a long time. Being around her wasn't difficult. I was 36 at the time, and had an opportunity to get to know many quality women, but there was something different about her. I'd been praying for a wife for over eighteen years. Had God finally answered my prayers?

We had an opportunity to talk about my mom and her condition. I found out that her father had passed away over a year ago of esophageal cancer, so she related to what I was going through. At the time, I'd been introduced to many books on healing and was confidant God would heal my mom. I got up on my soapbox a bit about it. Jodi was astute and asked me the question, "What if your mom isn't healed?"

I didn't realize it at the time, but the question would make or break my chances to woo her romantically. I realized that in the greatness of God, I couldn't reduce the issue to just plain faith. My answer to her: "God is sovereign and he has the ultimate say." I later found out that the answer proved to her that my theology and I weren't odd or unacceptable.

After spending the whole morning and afternoon together, Jodi invited me to join she and her friends for a movie. I was more than open

Praying with Mom

to extending our time together, but I had dinner plans with my Professor and his wife—though I'm sure they would've been fine had I canceled to have dinner with Jodi.

Following dinner, I went to her friend's room and met some current students. We watched a movie, but I was mostly enjoying the extended time with her. I felt so much peace around her. We'd been together all morning and afternoon, and here I was sitting next to her watching a movie on the same evening. My heart was at rest, a good opportunity to ask for her contact information.

I'd been on dates with women—wonderful, godly, beautiful women—but afterward, I felt tired and drained. (Likely, there were also women tired and drained by me as well.) There was something different about this. Jodi felt like an old friend. I'd just met her but easily spent the whole day with her. I really enjoyed her company and recognized something different about the woman.

I left the next day for home with something to look forward to. A few days later, at my friend's wedding, I attended the reception table with another young lady (also a set-up of sorts). Normally quite comfortable and outgoing, I felt a bit numb and tongue-tied. I had another friend who was aware of the situation and kept peering over toward the table. She and her husband commented that I seemed to have no spark or interaction. I told her how I met a young lady a few days before, and how something so different about her struck me above other women I'd met. More experiences and circumstances began to separate Jodi from others.

The great evangelist, George Whitefield, came to the States in the 18th century and met the great American Theologian, Jonathan Edwards. Many things impressed Whitefield of Edwards and one thing that impressed him was Edward's wife, Sarah. Whitefield would write in his journal:

> She is a woman adorned with a meek and quiet spirit, talked feelingly and solidly of the things of God, and seemed to be such a helpmate for her husband, that she caused me to renew those prayers, which, for some months, I have put up to God, that he would be pleased to send me a Daughter of Abraham to be my wife.
>
> 'I find, upon many accounts, it is my duty to marry. Lord I desire to have no choice of my own. Thou knowest my circumstances; thou knowest I only desire to marry in and for thee. 'Thou didst choose a Rebecca for Isaac, choose one for me to be a help-meet

for me, in carrying on that great work committed to my charge. Lord, hear me, Lord, let my cry come unto thee.[8]

I had this desire too. For many years, over eighteen of them at this point in life, I prayed for a mate, one handpicked by God. Had I met God's match?

Mom was still sick and my heart, though excited about Jodi, didn't possess the emotional energy that's needed to wholeheartedly pursue someone. It wasn't until a month and a half later that we'd interact again.

ENDNOTES

1. Romans 1:1.
2. Genesis 12:1–4
3. It has often been discussed that Ishmael was the progenitor of the Arabic race.
4. Genesis 22:5.
5. Hebrews 11:19.
6. Genesis 2:18.
7. As well as seeing grandchildren.
8. *George Whitefield's Journals.* (London: Banner of Truth Trust, 1965) 475-477. Unfortunately, George Whitefield did not have a good marriage. When he died, his wife did not find out till nine months later. A reminder that though we may desire marriage, the wrong one is worse than singleness.

12

When the Unexpected Changes Your Life

Jesus answered him, "What I am doing you do not understand now, but afterward you will understand."

—John 13:7

You find peace by coming to terms with what you don't know.

—Nassim Nicholas Taleb

As a disciple of Jesus Christ I must learn the discipline of change. My preconceived ideas of God's direction will be upset frequently because I am only God's servant, not His Counselor.

—W. Glyn Evans

Life changes. Khaled Hosseini's first novel, *The Kite Runner*, which became an international best seller and a movie in 2007, tells the story about a well to do family living in Afghanistan. When the Soviet Union invaded, this affluent and prominent family lost everything overnight.[1] The story showed how the wealthy man and his son fled Afghanistan to Fremont, California. They went from a huge mansion one day to a small apartment another. The father abruptly moved from a lucrative lifestyle

When the Unexpected Changes Your Life

of wealth and servants to working at a gas station. On weekends to make extra money, they sold goods at a flea market in San Jose. The story illustrates how suddenly and dramatically life changes. Some change happens expectedly, simply from the natural passage of time. Infants learn to walk. Children start school. High school students prepare to leave for college. People marry, have children, change jobs, retire. Life is full of expected change.

Life is also full of the unexpected. Dreams shatter. Health is lost. Relationships deteriorate, and trust is betrayed. The economically rich suddenly lose a large part of their assets due to market crashes. A woman preparing for her wedding suddenly loses her fiancé due to infidelity, fear, or a sudden fatality. Someone faithful to a company for years suddenly gets informed that the job will soon be terminated. A couple anticipating a home filled with children finds out they are infertile and never able to conceive their own. A loved one is murdered or commits suicide. People abruptly move due to a new job, loss of a job, or in order to better care for those they love. Healthy people suddenly discover a terminal diagnosis. Life changes suddenly and unexpectedly, which can forever alter our course.

Believers in Christ often feel they need to experience a life of victory, peace and undisturbed joy. A life where great things happen and great things are attempted. Certainly, this isn't foreign to the life of Christ followers. The Apostle Paul wanted to know Christ in the power of his resurrection. Everyone loves to see the power of God displayed, especially in their own lives, but Paul is balanced and recognizes that life isn't *all* victory, triumph, and power. His main ambition was to know Christ, not just in resurrection power, but also in fellowship with his suffering.[2] This ambition of Paul in regard to knowing Christ is rarely shared inside the church as a whole. Change is often the instrument used by God to experience sharing Christ's suffering. The pain of change is necessary if character formation towards Christ-likeness is to arise.[3]

People can be miserable if change is resisted. Humankind naturally desires comfort, ease, and happiness. Sometimes our views and expectations are skewed about who Jesus is and what he does. God is more concerned about our character than our comfort. Christ-likeness, in the long run, brings about more happiness than short-term circumstances of ease. We must remind ourselves not to despise or be unwelcoming of

Praying with Mom

pain that comes through change and believe God has a plan. Pain has its purpose and is often used to break down our spirit and soul in order to make us stronger than before.[4]

QUICK TRIP

My mother and I received some bad news. My aunt, who we'd seen a few months earlier, suddenly died in a car accident. An excerpt from the email I sent out read:

> Dear family in Christ,
> This world has a way of reminding us that it's not our home, we're just passing through. The groans of this imperfect world continue to besiege us, but there's a better one to come (Rom. 8:18–28).
> On Monday night, Oct. 9, my aunt was killed suddenly in a car crash in Cincinnati. She'd just returned from China and we were planning on staying with her at her home in Ohio. The news came as a shock to all the family as my aunt was only 67 and in good health. But, it's a reminder that life is short, and we're not guaranteed tomorrow and must make the most of the time God has given us to do his will (Psalm 90:12). Just a few months earlier my aunt and I were praying with my mom. My aunt asked God to give my mom at the very least ten more years to live. My mom jokingly lashed at my aunt for praying such a low number of years. Now, my aunt has gone before my mom and the rest of the family home to heaven. Praise God she knew the Lord and is with HIM now.
> My mom remains strong in her sadness, firm in her grief. But she and I can use prayer as God has allowed us to experience a lot of challenges this year.

One of my aunt's friends was a cardiologist and reviewed the police and coroner reports. He concluded that my aunt had a major heart attack while driving in her car. She'd always seemed healthy. Doctors in the hospital commented about her organs seeming very young, but her heart wasn't well. She did enjoy eating fatty foods, especially fatty pork but wasn't too overweight.

My mother and I boarded a plane for Ohio to speak at her funeral. It was odd, almost surreal to be going to Ohio. My aunt was in perfect health when she came to visit. Mother was the one terminally ill. We all prayed for my mother to be healed. There were even plans for my aunt to live with my mom if God would heal her of her cancer. But, as James writes, "You say, 'Today or tomorrow we will go into such and such a town and spend a year there and trade and make a profit'—yet you do not know what tomorrow will bring. What is your life? For you are a mist that appears for a little time and then vanishes. Instead you ought to say, 'If the Lord wills, we will live and do this or that.'"[5]

AN EMERGENCY LANDING

On the way to Ohio from California, our plane had to make an emergency landing in Indianapolis, Indiana. Someone on the plane was lying flat on the ground. Fortunately, a doctor was on board and began administering CPR. Flight attendants ran all over the cabin and people peered into the middle of the plane as the medical doctor worked tirelessly to save the man's life. Upon landing in Indiana, an EMS team boarded the plane and took the man away. I never knew what happened to him, but I did get to see his body pass by my aisle as the EMS team moved him out of the plane. He looked as if he'd suffered a sudden heart attack. I don't know if he survived. All I can say was his body seemed lifeless as it passed by in the aisle of the plane. Hopefully, he survived, but it was another reminder that life changes suddenly, often with little or no warning.

MAKING IT TO OUR DESTINATION

The plane took off from Indiana, and we made it to Ohio. Ohio was home to me, where I grew up and established my first roots. It was nice to be there and see old friends, but it was sad to say goodbye to my aunt.

The service was held at a small funeral home in Cincinnati, Ohio. People gathered together to pay final respects. One by one, people shared. I was responsible for the message. After I spoke, my mother came up to share. It was clear that the Spirit came upon her. The room was electric. She vulnerably shared stories of their childhood: how they were estranged, how they forgave each other, how they planned to grow old. Laughter mixed with tears was the reaction. Above all, Jesus was glorified. Although a very sad circumstance occurred, God was able to use it for good.[6] Not only did we remember my aunt, people heard the good news of how Christ suffered and died for the forgiveness of sin and conquered death by rising on the third day. People heard and saw clearly through what mom shared—Christ has come and will come again. Only in heaven will we truly know how things turn out. My mother shone light into a dark time. God used her to offer their story as sisters. Here's an email I sent in response to the service:

> *Dear family in Christ,*
>
> *We know God works all things for his good (Rom.8:28). Thank you so much for your prayers. Both the pastor and I were able to share at my aunt's funeral service. But, in my humble opinion, the most powerful sharing was from my mother. It was clear that people were tracking with her as I heard many laugh loudly then cry, as they were touched emotionally. My mom weaved in the gospel message in a simple manner and encouraged everyone to seek the Lord to be his or her Savior. I was very proud and blessed and grateful for your prayers. Two of my mom's friends want to come to church next week as my mom will be sharing again. Please pray for my mom to be used again as she will share on October 22 in a service that will honor the parents of those whose children are in full-time ministry.*
>
> *Thank you so much for your prayers, I know God has used them. Please pray for my mom to be used this Sunday as well for her physical and inner healing. I'm still persevering in faith and prayer (Luke 18:1) for her healing (Matt.8:16, 17) and rejoice that she has had opportunities to be used.*
>
> *With love and thanks,*
> *Mike*

Being in Ohio for my aunt's funeral wasn't easy, but God used it for good. Mom shared beautifully about spiritual, personal, funny and sad moments. She shared about Christ and glorified his name. Many people were touched by mom's words. God gave her a gift and this wasn't the last time she used it. Throughout her diagnosis, God opened doors for her to share and be useful.

We were in Ohio suddenly and without warning. God's ways are higher than ours. We don't always understand what he's doing, but we can trust that he has the best in mind for us. Our lives had changed. God had more in store for us than to pay our last respects to my aunt.

ENDNOTES

1. They have servants to help them , the main part of the story is the relationship of Amir, whose father is wealthy and prominent with his half-brother Hassan, who is the son of the servant of the house and who is close friends with Amir.
2. Philippians 3:10.
3. John 3:30
4. Rom. 5:1–8; Gal 4:19
5. James 4:13–15
6. Romans 8:28

13

Unpredicted Friends

Keep on loving each other as brothers. Do not forget to entertain strangers, for by so doing some people have entertained angels without knowing it.

—Hebrews 13:1–2

Beware in your prayers, above everything else, of limiting God, not only by unbelief, but by fancying that you know what he can do. Expect unexpected things, above all that we ask or think. Each time, before you Intercede, be quiet first, and worship God in his glory. Think of what he can do, and how he delights to hear the prayers of his redeemed people. Think of your place and privilege in Christ, and expect great things!

—Andrew Murray

Nassim Nicholas Taleb wrote an influential book titled *The Black Swan*. Written in 2007, Taleb predicted the economic crash of 2008. The title illustrates the point. If people only see white swans, then the notion that "all swans are white" is what's believed. The discovery of a black swan would nullify the statement.[1] Taleb's thesis is that the world we live in is more complex and uncertain than we think; for example, take a turkey. If the turkey is fed for one thousand days and is very fat and happy, then the turkey may conclude that those doing the feeding do it out of goodness

Unpredicted Friends

to the turkey and a desire to make it happy. The reality is that on day one thousand and one, the turkey is killed and eaten. This illustrates that the world is complex and uncertain.

Taleb states that a Black Swan is an unpredictable event that causes great change when it happens. Because people think the way that they do, Black Swans are explained away as if they're understood and predictable. There are positive Black Swans like penicillin and the computer, which were discovered totally by accident, as well as negative Black Swans, like a natural disaster which change the world and how we perceive it. [2]

TURNING DIFFICULTY INTO OPTIMISM

My mother and I were in Ohio for my aunt's funeral. It was obviously a sad occasion, but God had already used it to share his good news. Though the reason for our gathering was somber, blessings flowed among old friends and family, and being with everyone was so pleasant.

Mother never planned to return to Ohio. She scheduled a trip to Ohio six months after her diagnosis basically to say good-bye to people. Five months later, she came back.

AN EMAIL OUT OF THE BLUE

God had already convinced me about my negative attitude toward the Amish people. He was about to offer personal experience with one to offer me hope. I received this email while mom and I were in Cincinnati:

> "Dear friends,
> I have an attachment which you might find interesting. It is about an Amish man named Solomon Wickey. What is written about him by others is absolutely fascinating!
> Take care,
> J."

I'd heard about this man before this, but because of my issues with the Amish I didn't even consider seeing the man.[3] Overall, I thought the Amish people were secretive, odd and stale, but two weeks prior God had showed me I was wrong.

After receiving the email, I asked my mom if she was interested in seeing this man. Surprisingly, she said yes. Since we were already in

85

Cincinnati, not California, we were less than a three hour drive from Auburn, Indiana, where Solomon resides. At the time, he only saw people Monday to Wednesday. Tuesday and Wednesday were by appointment only. Monday was a walk-in day. So, I made arrangements for us to stay in a hotel in Auburn, and on Sunday mother and I drove to be near for a walk-in Monday morning.

HOPE REVIVED

Mother and I had visited institutions that were highly rated. At Stanford Hospital my mother's primary doctor was a very well known, respected oncologist. She was also seen at MD Anderson in Houston, Texas, which is usually rated as the top hospital in the nation for cancer treatment. People told my mom that the doctor treating her at MD Anderson was the best in the department. MD Anderson is part of the Texas Medical Center, a very large place that's famous for research and treatment. Yet here I was driving to a rural city to take my mom to see someone who doesn't even use electricity. Was I crazy?

SURREAL INDIANA EXPERIENCE

It was a cool, October morning. The sun hadn't risen and the rural area was almost pitch black. Cars lined up and were asked not to approach Wickey's house until 6am, fearing other neighbors' complaint. We arrived at Solomon Wickey's house that Monday morning and were led into a waiting room which was filled with people from all over the country. Some had seen Mr. Wickey before; others had heard about him and were there for the first time. Even area hotels had directions to his house. Some offered discounts if the purpose was to see the Amish man. Around 8am, we were informed that it was our turn. I thought I was in a movie as we entered the room. Solomon put an herb jar on my mother's leg and did some kinesiology tests. His conclusion: she doesn't have cancer.

I was stunned. Could he be right? Doctors had already diagnosed mom with stage 4 lung cancer. Her life expectancy was less than a year. Now, in a room with no electricity, lit with lamps and heated by kerosene stove, this Amish man said that my mom didn't have cancer. My mother was experiencing back pain. Solomon said that she had slipped discs.

After I heard the news, I told Mr. Wickey that I had everyone in the world praying for my mom, but I wasn't aware of anyone Amish praying for her. Mr. Wickey responded, "Well, now you do." I left his home that day with a renewed hope that mother would be fine.

INCONGRUENT DATA

The kind Amish man said there was no cancer. He also said mom's back would feel better, but pain continued. Was Wickey wrong?

We returned to California and went to Stanford Medical for more tests. Tests came back stable, but due to her back pain the doctor wanted to begin treatment. I was conflicted. I had great hope because of Mr. Wickey. Visiting him spurred me to call and email people who'd also seen Mr. Wickey. After all of my interviews and research, I concluded that he was used to helping others. I went back to California fully expecting confirmation, but I got the opposite. Instead, the doctor wanted to begin immediate treatment, and mom's back pain didn't get better. Here's an email I sent:

> Dear family in Christ,
> Yesterday we received the results of the PET Scan. The news wasn't good as the doctor said there's slight growth in the lining of my mom's left lung, as well as spreading to a bone in her back. My mom has been in great pain over her back at night and went immediately to chemotherapy. I couldn't believe I was there again after not being there for six months. It was like a bad dream. I really believed that God was about to move. He allowed me to interact with people I never would've had the chance to meet. After interacting with them, I felt God was moving towards healing. So the news yesterday was something I wasn't expecting. I didn't understand.
> I wrestled a while asking why. God lead me to Abraham in Gen 22. After waiting 25 years for the promised offspring that would produce descendents numbering the stars in the sky and having a chance to raise him, God called Abraham to sacrifice his son, the promised one who would give birth to Israel. It didn't make sense, but God uses things that don't make sense to test our faith. Abraham passed (Gen 22:12). I hope I can follow.

I felt floored. We'd just returned from Ohio, and I was given news that mom didn't have cancer. I believed that the medical results would confirm. Instead, my mother was again undergoing treatment, and I was again left wondering why. I thought she was on the road to healing, yet the medical evidence showed conflicting results. The roller coaster continued. I was given brief hope in Indiana only to have it dashed when we returned to California. Not only was mom not healed, but they also said it had spread to her back and radiation was a possibility.

HOPE AND COMFORT IN THE MIDST OF DESPAIR

God knew my soul was nearly crushed and had his plan to restore me. I emailed a friend to see if there was a Bible study to join. He emailed back and shared that their church was holding a retreat. The speaker happened to be my old professor from seminary. It was he, his wife and his wife's friend that were instrumental in setting up the meeting with Jodi. Now, he was in California speaking for the retreat at my friend's church. The timing couldn't have been more perfect. I'd reached my low point and was on the brink of despair. God knew and brought the Professor across the country. I told mother that my professor was in town. She told me to go to the retreat, because she'd be fine.

The weekend was an amazing time. God used the time to both encourage and offer me hope that God's plan is bigger. I went to a small chapel on the retreat grounds and prayed a sobbing prayer. I once again surrendered to God's timing and plan. I thought the meeting with Mr. Wickey would be the start of complete healing, but the results were different than I'd hoped. Now, I was again at the foot of the cross bearing heart and soul to the Lord, laying down my own agenda for his. Being with my professor, sharing this part of my soul with him while listening to his counsel were all needed encouragement. It was a life changing time that refueled lost, much needed energy.

I still remember taking walks with my professor during the weekend talking about life. There was really nothing specific that he said which moved me, simply being together having fellowship ministered to me. Being around so many men praising and worshipping, God helped refocus my mind on the sovereignty and goodness of God. His plan was perfect despite any of my setbacks.

ROMANCE IGNITED

A month and a half passed since Jodi and I met in Boston. Because of the intense emotion involved in mom and I's situation, dealing with the ups and downs of my aunt's passing, meeting Mr. Wickey, then hearing conflicting reports, I'd not had the emotional energy to invest in pursuing romantic interest with Jodi or risk the rejection. As the weekend closed I felt it was time to take a chance and call. My professor had encouraged my heart so much that I entered a place of knowing I needed to go on living. He encouraged me to initiate more with her.

I saved Jodi's number before I left Boston in September and hoped to call it. Now, a month and a half later, I finally dialed. Did she already find someone else? Is she not interested? How would she respond? Was I wasting time? Initiation is always a challenge and a risk. I knew I needed to take it.

God used Jodi's presence. After receiving the bad news from the doctors about the cancer spreading, I remember having lunch with mom, trying to hold back tears. I was about to lose it when I told my mother that I'd met someone in Boston. Mother was very interested. I described how we met and the connection, how I wanted to get to know her better. At that moment sharing about Jodi helped refresh and prevent me from bursting into tears in front of mom. Now, I was about to call Jodi to see if our story would continue.

I dialed and was pleased that Jodi responded well. She seemed interested and asked many questions. It was about an hour-long phone conversation, but it didn't seem like it. I sensed she was interested and began my pursuit.

SOME MORE GOOD NEWS

Romance, though exciting, wasn't my primary focus. I took time to pray and fast about mom's condition. She was in the process of possibly starting radiation. After her treatment, her back pain immediately left. This caused the doctors to reassess their diagnosis. After much study and consultation, they determined that what they thought was spreading to the back was wrong, so radiation treatment was cancelled. I rejoiced and sent out this email:

> *Dear family in Christ,*
> *Some good news. Mom went in to prepare for radiation treatment. Her back had been in pain for over one month and thats what caused mom to have scans and ushered her back into treatment. My mom's back has been feeling better the last five days.*

Praying with Mom

> *The doctor said that the initial glance at mom's scans on Monday show improvement, and that if my mom continues to feel well and her back pain doesn't increase, then radiation won't be done.*
>
> *God has shown me that I continually need to be surrendered. I realized my prayers were directed towards me and not God. I appealed to God for healing because I didn't want to lose my mom. But that's not what prayer is for. It's not meant for me to get what I want, but for me to know and love and trust God. Hence, I have experienced much more peace recently as I've become more surrendered to the will of God and realize there's an aspect of HIS will that's mysterious (Deut. 29:29). His ways are higher (Isaiah 55).*

My soul was filled joy. God used unexpected friends to ignite a hopeful heart. We'd met Mr. Wickey a month ago, and although the medical results didn't match his diagnosis, there was hope that mother's time on earth wasn't finished. Then, out of the blue, I got to spend more time with the professor that God used so mightily in my life. Spending time with him showed me that I needed to make a call. Romance would begin with Jodi, but it would be three months before we'd meet again. God provided friends for me at unexpected times as part of his sovereign plan to comfort and move me to take each new step.

Mother was doing better. We continued to pray at night. Our prayers were always similar: healing, surrender, etc. The real blessing for me continued to be praying with mom. With Jodi and the good news about mom's health, there was much to pray about.

ENDNOTES

1. Taleb states that a black swan was discovered in Australia. See Nassim Taleb *The Black Swan: The Impact of the Highly Improbable* (New York: Random House, 2007).

2. As of 2011, the world has seen Japan endure a major earthquake and tsunami which threatens their nuclear power plants, floods and tornadoes have ravaged the USA to name a few.

3. For more information regarding Solomon Wickey, see the books: June Naugle *Solomon's Touch: The Life and Work of Solomon J. Wickey* (Bloomington, IN: AuthorHouse, 2005) and Tenna Merchant *He's Not Autistic, But . . .* (Noblesville, IN: Joyous Messaenger, Inc., 2007)

14

Romance and Respite

The light of the eyes rejoices the heart, and good news refreshes the bones.
—Proverbs 15:30

Take a rest; a field that has rested gives a bountiful crop.
—Ovid

"It was the best of times, it was the worst of times . . . it was the spring of hope, it was the winter of despair," opens Charles Dickens's *A Tale of Two Cities*. The classic line summed up my experience. When mother had bad news—growth of her tumor, possible spreading, pain in her back—it was the worst of times. When the news was good—shrinkage, stable, good response to medicines, lack of pain—it was the best of times. After meeting my professor in California and mustering up the courage to call Jodi, life began to change. Mother entered a season of good news. Consistently, I sent out emails praising God. Mother was doing well, which meant I was doing well.

> *Dear family in Christ,*
> *Some good news, my mom went in to prepare for radiation treatment. Her back had been in pain for over one month. That's what caused mom to get scans and start treatment. My mom's back has been feeling better the last five days.*

Praying with Mom

> *The doctor said that his initial glance at mom's scans on Monday showed improvement, and if she continues to feel well and her back pain doesn't increase, then he won't do radiation.*
>
> *Though I believe God wants to heal (Matt. 8:17) and desires us to be whole (1 Thess. 5:23–24). I know that his way is not always comprehensible to humankind. But, he is totally trustworthy (2 Tim. 2:13), and his way is perfect (Rom. 12:1–2). There's so much more peace when we rest in the Lord (Isaiah 26:3) not expecting God to answer prayer just so that we get what we want.*

A TIME TO REST

Weeks passed and mom's back didn't hurt. She went into a season where scans were mainly stable or showing shrinkage. This was music to my ears and good medicine for my soul.[1]

God was also stirring up unexpected romance. I was calling Jodi once a week. We usually talked about an hour or more. It was easy to talk to her, but I was still cautious. Being older, I'd experienced hopeful relationships in the past that, much to my dismay, didn't work out. As time passed I began to wonder if I'd ever find someone to marry. Now, I called Jodi regularly, and she responded well. Life became more restful. Mom got better and there was great hope. Good news continued:

Dear family in Christ,

The doctors reviewed the recent scans and have concluded that there's no cancer in my mother's back. Radiation has been cancelled. My mother's back has been in great pain the last few months, but it's been improving. She no longer needs medication at night to combat the pain.

My soul rejoiced. I love my mother very much, and to see her struggle broke my heart; to see her do well and have hope that God wasn't finished with her made my soul happy.

FEARFUL OF REJECTION

From the time my professor came to speak in California—one, personal low point—God orchestrated change. I called Jodi shortly after and continued to call her weekly over the next three months. She lived in Houston. I was with mom in the San Francisco area. I was always nervous before I called. Rejection is something all men fear.[2] That's why it's sometimes

Romance and Respite

hard for men to initiate relationships with women at all. Rejection hurts. Rather than putting oneself on the line, some take the easy route and don't take initiative to get to know others. Fearing rejection caused nervousness before each call, but I also knew it was worth the risk.

Humankind yearns for acceptance, we long to be loved, to be understood, and to be important. Jesus wasn't always accepted. In fact, rejection was common to him. As Jesus grew, he had favor with God and humankind.[3] However, once he began his ministry his family and neighbors from his hometown tried to throw him off a cliff.[4] Jesus wasn't preoccupied with being accepted but with pleasing his father. As his disciples, we follow.[5]

Acceptance and favor from the world don't go hand-in-hand with the message of the Gospel. The world doesn't want to repent and believe that Jesus saves people from their sin. No one enjoys being told they're wrong.

Romantic rejection is different. Unlike being rejected for following Christ and sharing his life and message, romantic rejection stings a different way. Romantic rejection is a rejection of one's self which makes it difficult to initiate with others.

Women, like men, long to know they're appreciated and special. It's important for men like me to look beyond ourselves and step forward to let a woman know she's important. Each time I called Jodi, I worried whether she'd respond well to me.

A SURPRISE VISIT AND SWEET REUNION

It turns out that Jodi was coming to the Bay area for her grandmother's 94th birthday celebration. She emailed and told me the plans for her trip, and I communicated that I looked forward to seeing her. News from Jodi also encouraged mom's heart. She remembered the first time I mentioned Jodi to her at the In-n-Out Burger. I was about to cry from recent doctor reports when I diverted to telling mom about the young lady in Boston that I'd met, how friends set us up, and the chemistry between us. She remembered my hope to learn more about her. Even the first mention had made mom happily intrigued while it prevented me from crying. Mom and I were in a new season of joy. She had hope that her son would eventually marry, and I was hopeful that mom would heal.

Praying with Mom

Jodi and her mom flew into the Bay Area on a Thursday evening. Friday morning I left mom's house and drove to meet Jodi for the second time. I arrived and her uncle answered the door. Six months had passed since I saw Jodi. She looked really beautiful.

After brief introductions and discussion, Jodi and I left on a second date. We spent the day making chocolate at a Napa Valley cooking institution. Then, that night we ate at a Korean restaurant and watched a movie at an old-time movie theater in Berkeley. It was a fun day. Once again, the thing that struck me was how easy it was for me to be around her. We were together almost thirteen hours, and I wasn't the least bit tired.

The day was coming to an end, and I had to drop my date back at her uncle's house. I knew the next day would be her grandma's birthday party. Would I be invited? An invitation would be a sign that the family approved of me and were open for me to romance Jodi. Her uncle greeted us at the door, and before I left he extended the invitation. I was excited! When I told my mom I'd been invited, she was excited too. She knew an invitation to the party would be a good sign. I'd be the only person that wasn't family or close friends. Mom knew it signaled that the family was approving of me. An invite as an outsider to an important event was a great honor for me, and I looked forward to spending more time with Jodi.

I met the family at a Chinese restaurant in Oakland. Everyone wondered who I was and what I was doing there. Family photos of the event elicited comments of "who is this guy"? Overall the weekend was a very good one. Jodi spent more time with me than she did with her family. She shared that one of the reasons she wanted to come to the Bay Area was to spend time with me.

The whole weekend was a fun time, refreshing for my soul. We were together three days, and I didn't tire at all of being together. After our weekend together we said goodbyes, and then I told her I'd see her next week. Mother and I were scheduled at MD Anderson in Houston. Jodi lived in Houston. God was perfectly orchestrating our romance.

HOUSTON, THERE IS NO PROBLEM

A week passed. Mom and I boarded the plane for Houston, Texas and MD Anderson. We checked into our hotel then went to mom's friend's house for a visit. I left early to have dinner with Jodi's family where I met her brother, sister-in-law, nephew and niece. The dinner went well, and the week in Houston picked up where the time in California had ended. Mother and I stayed at MD Anderson during the day, and I spent time with Jodi in the evenings.

Our moms seemed to sense something in the air. Mom was asked to speak at the church in Houston where Jodi's family attended. Jodi's mom came to listen. They scheduled a luncheon together afterward to get to know each another better. Their connection was natural and easy, and a good relationship developed between them. Mom brought up the issue of financing our wedding, but one issue stood in mom's way: we hadn't officially begun dating yet.

MAKING IT 'OFFICIAL'

After the week together it was clear that something needed to be said. I preached at Jodi's church from Psalm 42:5. My soul had been downcast throughout mom's diagnosis and the best antidote was putting hope in God. He has the power to change things, and he has the plan. I don't always understand his ways, but I need to put my hope in him.[6] The sermon was based on my experience with mom; the ups and downs and the hardship of seeing someone I loved so much suffer. Many people talked with me and thanked me for the message. Jodi's pastor asked me to come and serve with the church.

Things were looking up. Mom continued to be well and looked great. She and Jodi's mom connected and became friends. Now, someone was asking me to serve in their church? Things were changing. Although my soul was still struggling, the circumstances surrounding everything eased up. Tears still often streamed down my face, but at least there was hope that mom would be around for a while. There was also hope that I might marry. If someone had asked what my two biggest prayer requests were, it would've been for mom's health and a mate. God was answering both.

After the Sunday sermon and lunch, Jodi and I took a walk in a nearby park. Nervous to tell her that I wanted to court her, we walked a few minutes and came to a picnic table largely secluded. I asked her to sit down, took a deep breath, and told her how I felt. I told her how easy it was to be around her, how much I enjoyed time together, and how great I thought she was. I shared that I wanted our relationship to be more than just friends, and I committed to seeing where God led our relationship. I also told her that I wasn't interested in dating other women. I only wanted to see if God led us closer together. She felt the same way. We talked a little longer, prayed, and when we left the picnic table, I held out my hand to hold hers. We walked out of the park hand in hand. It began a journey of love for both of us.

CONTINUED STABILITY

Mom's week at MD Anderson didn't turn up any new results. I hoped that tests would show no cancer, but she left MD Anderson the same. In coming weeks, mom continued to improve or remain stable. I still had hope that God would completely heal my mom and continued to pray for healing. She began another clinical trial. I sent out this email:

> *Dear family in Christ,*
>
> *My mom will begin a clinical trial. I rejoice that my mom is doing well. She sounds better and people often comment that she looks great and has a lot of spunk. Even though this has been so hard, I rejoice that my mom is doing well and that there's no evidence she's going "home" anytime soon. I pray this experience empowers her to use her gifts for the Kingdom (Eph.4:16).*
>
> *I know your prayers are a large part of my mother doing so well (2 Cor.1:11). Many of you have been faithfully praying for my mom for this past year and a half (Eph.6:18). Your love and support have made a difference, and I thank you for them.*
>
> *Again, the trials have been hard and part of me would love for it to end, but I press on believing God and thanking him for his goodness to me this past year and a half.*

Mother was in the trial for almost one year. Her back didn't hurt and her growth showed much improvement. The nurses and doctors told her that she was the star. Her growth shrank by as much as thirty percent at one point during the trial. I was always happy to receive good news, and the period following my courtship with Jodi proved to be one filled with good news. Mother hoped for grandchildren together with the potential daughter-in-law.

Mom was always concerned about her children and their future. She was afraid that if she went to heaven, we wouldn't be taken care of. It was her nature to want the best for her kids and to protect them. Now, I was dating, and she sensed that I'd be well taken care of. Her desire was always for me to marry; she knew her life purpose wasn't to forever watch over me.

I believe the greatest gift a parent gives their children is the security that their parents love them. I never doubted for a second that mom loved me. Was she perfect? No. Do I wish she would've done some things differently and made better choices? Yes, but every human is flawed, and we need grace not only from God but also from those who love us. I needed grace toward my mom in areas that she wasn't perfect. One area that needed no grace was the area of loving. I have no doubt that mom loved me. Because love is the greatest entity we can experience or be deprived of, losing those we love can cause excruciating pain.

MOVING TO HOUSTON

Since mother was doing so well, I decided it was time to see if Jodi was someone I could marry. I moved to Houston, and my brother moved to San Francisco from Los Angeles to support mom. Mother entered a period of great news. Prayers were answered, and she seemed to be on the road to healing. I was hoping and praying mom would live to see grandchildren and be able to love them. But first things first, I had to see if Jodi was indeed the one to marry. Being a doctoral student allowed some freedom to change locations. Mother graciously helped with expenses during my study and courtship. Jodi and I began dating, and I relocated to Houston at the end of April.

My days were spent studying and preparing sermons. Jodi worked full-time as a youth minister in the church. Both of us had a similar calling and vision for life. I'm convinced that God uses significant relationships in our lives to shape our character. God used my dating relationship to grow many areas of weakness.

UPS AND DOWNS OF COURTSHIP

Some people need relationships all the time. I recall various men and women that always had a girlfriend or boyfriend. Sometimes dating is selfish. People enter into relationships to fight the void from loneliness and insecurities.

My philosophy was that when people "date" someone, the purpose is to find a mate. Some people believe a person should know within one or two dates if another person is worth the time and energy of dating. A wise man told me, "if you doubt, don't."

Jodi and I weren't dating for our own needs. We made it clear that our purpose was to see if God would lead us into marriage. I was in my thirties when we first began dating.[7] Getting to know someone isn't easy. As beautiful, handsome, wonderful and godly as someone is, everyone has faults and flaws. No one is perfect. Jodi was everything: beautiful, godly, quality character, intelligent, competent, dependable, and beloved by many. Still, we both brought into the relationship issues of imperfection. God used each of us to begin smoothing these areas out in one another.

Because of these issues, our time of courtship wasn't always smooth. I think both of us got used to the idea that we could marry or not after waiting for so long. There were times when both of us questioned if our relationship worked. There was part of me that sensed that Jodi was the one. She stood out from the beginning, but then rocky times came.

We had similarities and our differences. One thing I noticed, she took in information more through her senses while I was more intuitive.[8] How did we differ in just this one area?

> Sensing (S) versus Intuition (N)
>
> This indicates whether a learner prefers to perceive the world by directly observing the surrounding reality or through impressions and imagining possibilities.
>
> Sensing people choose to rely on their five senses. They are detail-oriented, they want facts, and they trust them. Sensing learners prefer organized, linear, and structured lectures (systematic instruction or step-by-step learning).
>
> Intuitive people seek out patterns and relationships among the facts they have gathered. They trust hunches ("sixth" sense) and their intuition and look for the "big picture." They also value imagination and innovation. Intuitive learners prefer various forms of discovery learning and must have the big picture (metaphors and analogies), or an integrating framework in order to understand a subject. They like concept maps and/or often compare and contrast tables.[9]

The difference in this area posed some communication challenges. Couples with similar personality types, especially in the area of sensing versus intuition tend to communicate with each other more easily. We differed, so miscommunication was common. I was an N on this scale while she was an S, so this caused us to have to continually work on communication.

We faced other challenges. Attraction wasn't always there for her. The main reason Jodi felt an issue of attraction was mainly rooted in me. I felt insecure and rather than communicate feelings of vulnerability, I carried an air of confidence and "having it all together". I used the issue of my mom's drawn out diagnosis and seeing God be faithful as pillars of confidence in him. I put up a front.

Another issue was my physical health, I was close to 35 pounds overweight when Jodi and I began our relationship. I definitely needed to lose weight, not just for physical attractiveness but for my own fitness. Concerns of not easily communicating how I felt coupled with physical weight made it hard for Jodi to feel consistent in her attraction toward me. She confided in her close friends and prayed, asking God for guidance. God moved quickly.

One day, something stunned Jodi. She couldn't explain it. Her friends call it God moving. She felt an attraction for me she'd not felt for a while. One night I was thinking she wasn't even interested in talking to me, but later that evening, things changed. Jodi indicated to me that she felt strong attraction. The next morning, I thought it had worn off and she'd return to the earlier struggle with attraction. Instead, she greeted me at her mom's house communicating that she felt the same way. Things changed from that day forward.

A BOSTON PROPOSAL

Our relationship progressed and reached a point where decisions needed to be made. I asked the Lord to finally and clearly show me whether Jodi was the one I should marry. One of Jodi's friends was marrying in Boston, the site of our first date. My prayer was that he would make it clear on our trip whether or not I should propose. I had a pretty good idea already that I wanted to marry her, but in my heart I wanted the area surrendered to God and gave him more time to direct me. I prayed that our time in Boston would speak clearly about proposing.

We flew from Houston to Boston. I picked up the car at Logan airport, and we proceeded to drive to Rockport for dinner at the Roy Moore Seafood company, the site of our first lunch together. I stayed with a friend in Lexington. She stayed with a friend in Cambridge. It was a joyous and fun weekend together.

I always felt that vacationing together was an important sign of compatibility. Vacation and rest are important. If a couple can't vacation well together, then I felt it could mean there are varying values and life issues. The weekend was anything but difficult. I enjoyed the friend's wedding, walks around Boston with her, and vacationing together. After the weekend, I knew I wanted to propose.

THE PROPOSAL: SHE SAID . . .?

Every proposal story differs, some are dramatic, some aren't. Some are very extravagant, and others are very simple. A pastor once told me that the proposal is when the man shines, and the wedding ceremony is where the woman shines. In my heart I wanted a memorable proposal story, so I began to brainstorm. One idea: take Jodi to a building in Houston that overlooks the city and propose there. Another: a meal on a roof top—again overlooking the city. But, my real desire was to propose to Jodi in Boston, the place we'd first met, specifically, Rockport, Massachusetts. We had our first deep discussion over our first lunch together there at a certain spot. It was the place that I first felt Jodi may be the one to marry. The problem was how to get her to Boston without her anticipating what I wanted to do. It needed much prayer and help.

I called her pastor and close friends and shared my plan. The pastor gave me his blessing to take Jodi away to Boston to propose, and her friends were aware of the plan as well. I told Jodi there was an excellent deal on an engagement ring in Boston, but they would only do business in person (I never truly thought she'd believe that story). Somehow, Jodi agreed to go to Boston to shop for the engagement ring believing we were traveling to get a good deal on one—I'd actually already bought the engagement ring.

Romance and Respite

We left early morning from Houston to stay with the same people we'd been with when we traveled to Boston earlier for Jodi's friend's wedding. We landed at Logan airport and picked up the rental car. I worried that she'd find out what I was up to before I proposed, but God blinded her eyes and mind to what was happening. We drove to Rockport and walked to the Roy Moore Seafood company. At our table, a dozen roses symbolized the twelve months of knowing each other and seven white babies' breath symbolized the seven months of dating and courtship. As she spotted the bouquet she gave me a kiss. Her heart melted a little and maybe she began to anticipate something. We ordered lobster. She proceeded to tell me stories of how co-workers' spouses often sent flowers to the office after a fight. I wasn't offering reconciliation. I was hoping to prepare a moment to remember for the rest of our life.

We finished our meal and walked around. I led Jodi to the spot where we'd had our first deep conversation and I first thought I might marry her. I told her I loved her, got on one knee and asked her to marry me. On that cool New England evening in Rockport, Massachusetts in our very memorable spot that she'd first become special to me, Jodi said yes.

CALLING MOM

The first person we called was my mom. As soon as she heard the news that we were engaged, a loud and happy voice permeated the phone line. She lived to see her son engaged, soon to marry. What a blessing! At the beginning of her diagnosis, Jodi and I hadn't even met, no prospect of marriage. Mom had no hope that she'd live to see the day I had a wife. Now, almost two years since her diagnosis of a few months to live, mom was getting a daughter.

I needed this time. My soul was drying up and my heart sickening. The period of good news—of mom's health and a fiancée—poured needed life into my wearying heart and soul. Life filled with hope. Prayers of the saints were being answered. Mom was doing great. The doctor and nurses all commented that she was doing well. God led me to a beautiful woman as my future wife. I searched, longed and prayed for a mate from the age of eighteen (at least as far back that I can remember). God now answered the prayers. I'd done Internet services, been set-up, attended functions and events with hope of meeting someone, *but God* provided a life partner for me. A period of rest for my weary soul began. Tears didn't flow like the previous year. My heart had great hope that my and mother's best days weren't finished.

ENDNOTES

1. Proverbs 13:12.
2. I am conservative in this area and apologize to the women who feel they can initiate. My position on dating is that man needs to be the initiator and woman needs to be the responder, but women can drop hints to men they maybe interested in.
3. Luke 2:52.
4. Luke 4:28–29.
5. John 8:29.
6. Isaiah 55.
7. I will not tell you Jodi's age but I am older.
8. This is based on the personality test, Meyers-Briggs.
9. Taken from http://www.nwlink.com/~donclark/hrd/styles/jung.html

15

Wedding Day

A good marriage is the union of two forgivers.
—Ruth Graham

When I have learnt to love God better than my earthly dearest, I shall love my earthly dearest better than I do now.
—C.S. Lewis

House and wealth are an inheritance from fathers, But a prudent wife is from the LORD.
—Proverbs 19:14

It was eighteen years in the making, since my freshman year in college, prayers upon prayers had been poured out for a mate. Now, the day arrived. Had I written the story of my life, marriage would be a much earlier chapter. Fortunately, the story of my life wasn't up to me, God was doing the writing. I just walked with him as best as I could. After almost a year of dating and six month's engagement, my prayer for a spouse was answered.

Wedding ceremonies are some of the most memorable and glorious times in life, a culmination of years of waiting and praying, and months of planning. Hopefully, the two people entering the union select well, not just based on emotion and feeling but also facts and the approval of those around them. I knew Jodi was a woman of high character, she was valued by many with the respect of men and women I held in high regard.

I began to think about how life would be had I received my wish to marry earlier. At such a young age, I wouldn't have known myself very well and also wouldn't have understood the importance of selflessness in relationships. My motivation to marry early was mostly emotional. It was based on a desire to banish loneliness and wanting someone to satisfy my needs. These are not entirely selfish reasons, but I think if a person isn't mature enough to consider another's needs as equally and even more important than their own, marriage will be difficult. Disaster would've happened had the Lord allowed me to marry when I wanted. People who marry young can make a happy marriage. I see many around me who have married young and who are doing well, but for me, it wouldn't have been the best. Now, after years of waiting, I was going to make a vow for life to the woman I'd waited for.

On a sunny and warm Houston day I arrived at the church and proceeded to go to the dressing room to put on my tux. On the way to the dressing room I got a glimpse of the sanctuary where the wedding ceremony would take place. It looked beautiful, decorated with flowers all over the church. I was impressed. I waited for this day for so long. Finally it had come.

Beloved friends and family from all over the country—around the world—came to celebrate with us. I believe this is one major reason a wedding day is so special. Never again will the same group or this many friends and family gather in one place to celebrate.

Theologically, marriage came before the fall of humankind. God brought Eve to Adam because the Lord declared it not good for him to be alone. Unfortunately, Adam and Eve disobeyed God and caused the world to be in perpetual groaning.[1] Some people are called to be single; others choose singleness for the purpose of the Kingdom.[2] Over my thirty-five years of waiting, there were times I began to wonder if I'd ever meet someone I could marry.

In December of 2005 when my mom was first diagnosed, I wasn't dating anyone and hadn't met Jodi. My focus quickly changed from my life and pursuits to my mother's health. Mother became the priority of my life. The first year with mom's illness was the saddest year ever lived. Every morning I thanked God for another day with mom. Marriage was never a thought. I didn't think it'd happen in mom's lifetime because of

Wedding Day

her diagnosis. Now, almost two years and two months from the day I learned about mom's illness, she was gaining a daughter-in-law. Mother always wanted a daughter. She was thankful for two sons, but I know she would've enjoyed a daughter.

The best part of it all? Mom looked great and received great news from her doctors. She seemed to be getting better. I know and believe God used the prayers of the saints to help her.[3]

MAKING MARRIAGE OFFICIAL

My tux was on and I anxiously waited in the dressing room. I hadn't seen Jodi all day, but people were calling me and telling me how beautiful she looked. Brides are some of the most beautiful women, often adorned in beautiful wedding dresses with their faces aglow with joy and happiness. I couldn't wait to see her!

The minister officiating our ceremony came into the dressing room to pray with my groomsmen and I, then he led us into the sanctuary. I remember standing in eager anticipation, waiting for my bride to walk down that aisle. The ceremony began with bridesmaids, junior bridesmaids, family and flower girls all walking down the aisle. But, the one I was most eager to see hadn't appeared. Then it happened, I got the first glimpse of *my* bride. I was amazed at her beauty, grace, and elegance as she came down the aisle. My heart and soul were nothing but smiles.

The ceremony was filled with Scriptures, beautiful music, communion, singing, and vows. Many people commented that it was a beautiful service. After more than eighteen years of waiting, I was no longer single. God blessed me with a beautiful mate who loved him and loved me among the many respectable people that admired her. Many friends and family took time to join us and celebrate our union. It was one of the happiest moments in my life.

Mom was doing great, all smiles. We danced together at the reception, and she showed no sign of being tired. We did a mother–son dance, and mom showed off her moves during the evening. She was so happy; one of her fears was alleviated. She had hope that her son would be taken care of when she finished life here on earth.

I know that a mother's heart always desires the best for her children. Mom was at peace that her son married well and would be fine. Even though I was a grown man who'd been on my own for years, mom didn't have peace until I wed. Not only was she relieved that I had someone to care for me, she had hope for grandchildren.

My heart was overjoyed that mom was at the wedding. I had all the more faith that she was healed, her time with us wasn't too short nor God's plan for her life finished. I also thought everything was improving and would continue that direction. I thought the wedding day launched one of the happiest years of life. Mother was on her way to New Orleans to speak at a church as well as to groups at the University of Tulane. Everything was looking up, but as seen in the earlier chapters life has a way of being unpredictable.

ENDNOTES

1. Romans 8:18.
2. Matthew 19:12.
3. 2 Corinthians 1:11

16

Preparing to Say Goodbye

We all labor against our own cure, for death is the cure of all diseases.
—Thomas Browne

This world is the land of the dying; the next is the land of the living.
—Tryon Edwards

For to me, to live is Christ and to die is gain.
—Philippians 1:21

Life is a series of hellos and good-byes, new and old, beginnings and endings. I was beginning a new season of life, bachelorhood forsaken for matrimony. Mother was doing well and there was a chance she'd be around a while.

After the wedding ceremony, Jodi and I honeymooned in Hawaii. It was a special place filled with beauty and character all its own. The beaches were clear white, whales off the shore were visible to the eyes, and sea turtles often reared their heads near the shore. God's natural beauty was on display.

The honeymoon ended, and we entered back into "real life". It took some adjustment. For so long, the attention was on us. Preparations were made; gifts sent; people wished us well. The wedding ceremony happened, then the reception and all of life seemed to stop for the bride and groom. Next was the honeymoon where the newlywed couple spends every moment of every hour with each other for a period of time, usually one to two weeks—but sometimes longer or shorter.

Then, the honeymoon ends. The plane lands. Bags unpacked. Gifts unwrapped and life begins again. All of a sudden, the attention is over.

Jodi and I returned from our honeymoon, and I began to reflect on the last three years amazed at all that had happened. From the people we met to the things we experienced, then meeting a wife; all was used for God's glory. I thought the best was yet to be, but things in life don't always work out the way we hope.

The first bit of news that came was my mother's condition. I'd been married almost three months and mom decided she wanted to go to Taiwan to visit and participate in the inauguration of the new president. When she was first diagnosed, one of the thoughts that crossed her mind was that she'd not live long enough to see the new president of Taiwan elected. Now, almost three years later, she signed up for a tour to see the inauguration. Before the trip, her oncologist told her the growth in her lung had begun to grow and that the current treatment would be discontinued. He also told her not to worry and go on her trip.

The second bit of news that came was regarding my study. I hoped that my doctoral work would be completed soon after my marriage so I could find a job and provide for us. Unfortunately, the quality of my work wasn't ready, the recommendation was for me to take more time to work on it. Fortunately, I was at a point where my research was able to be thoroughly evaluated and clear suggestions were given to help get my work up to the standards necessary to finish. The worst was yet to come.

Mom returned from Taiwan in early June and felt very tired. I thought she'd be fine, but as the weeks passed she continued to be tired. The Beijing Olympics were about to begin and she didn't seem as excited as I thought she'd be. When she shared at churches, the Beijing Olympics were something she shared about being disappointed to miss if she passed away. Now they arrived, and although she was very happy to see it, I could tell she was more worn-out than usual. Scans later revealed that small growths had developed on her brain. She underwent treatment called Cyber-Knife where they projected a small laser beam directly at the nodules. Twice she underwent this procedure.

Scans also showed the growths spreading to her right lung. For almost three years, her scans revealed stable or slight growth or even shrinkage at times; but now, spreading to her brain and the other lung occurred. It was clear that mom was declining. I would not give up and continued to pray and pray and pray.

Mother came to Texas during Thanksgiving. It was such a joy to have her, but it was obvious that she didn't have the energy she once had. She often tired easily and had to lie down. Despite the decline, mother kept her spirits up and a few days after Thanksgiving, she shared at a small church in College Station, TX.[1] She got up and was very strong and eloquent. Her sharing made people laugh and cry and touched the hearts of many. Afterward they approached her and thanked her for the encouraging message she gave.

I was so proud to see her share so well and be used by God. I had hope that God would heal her and continue to use her to share in churches all among the Chinese-speaking world. Mother had a gift connecting to people's hearts while communicating biblical truth in simple ways. People understood her and related to her. I prayed mom's gift would be used more. Unfortunately, it was the last time she'd speak at a church.

Mom and my brother left. My brother said it was a great trip for my mom. My wife and I bought our tickets for Christmas. We planned to fly out to CA to be with my mom.

Christmastime is often a very happy time to celebrate the birth of Christ. It became even more special for me as I realized more frequently that time with loved ones is the most precious gift we have. Jodi and I flew out to the Bay Area in California to spend Christmas with my mom. We rang the doorbell. Mom answered the door. She looked great, her face beaming and radiant. Her appearance made me very happy, and I hoped there would be many more Christmases together. Mom was doing well the first few days we were there.

Friends from Houston—also in the Bay Area for a conference after Christmas from Dec.26-30—brought their own mother, who has battling pancreatic cancer, to the conference for prayer because of the stories of God moving mightily during the conferences healing people of various ailments. The conference was a powerful time of faith, prayer and inspiring stories. Young people changed life courses. Older people recommitted their faith and life to walk with God. Many sick people also came to the conference for prayer and healing. My mom was given a prayer counselor and the first thing he asked was, "Is there anyone she needed to forgive?" She said there was and shared with the counselor the person who had hurt her during the misunderstanding. She later shared with my mother-in-law how this was very helpful. The counselor prayed for my mom and led her in a prayer. After the conference, I sensed that my mom's spirit was better. I hoped that God would heal her, but God's ways are higher than ours.[2]

My newfound hope that mom would be healed was dashed the next morning. Mom called and asked me to take her to the emergency room. She was having trouble breathing. My spirit was crushed. She'd done so well at the conference. It was obvious her spirits were higher and her countenance brightened. We arrived at my mom's house, and I drove her to the hospital. X-rays were taken and she was put on oxygen. From that day forward, she was on an oxygen machine to help her breath. The next days and weeks were spent going in and out of hospitals. Mother needed a wheelchair to get around. My prayer life changed and exclusively focused on praying for mom's health again, still believing and holding hope that she would be healed. God had brought many things into my life over the years—good reports, people praying with vision, people receiving a word of insight or encouragement. Many signs pointed to mom being healed, but now, everything changed and her situation began to worsen. Only God could pull her through. Only God could help her. He was in control.

We saw my mom's oncologist soon after. The doctor didn't seem too concerned. I got the impression that she seemed to feel my mother would be around a while. Maybe it was overconfidence on mom's doctor's part because for years mom defied odds as well as often became the star patient among treatment groups. My heart was troubled. I emailed the prayer group, who faithfully prayed over three years, to ask them to continue praying for mom.

I was scheduled to leave Dec. 30, but I stayed for another week. After a few days, mother left the hospital, and we celebrated the New Year together. At first, I had hope. A few days after New Years mother wanted to go shopping. She didn't want to take her oxygen tank with her so she left it in the car and proceeded to walk all around the shopping market. I had my hand placed on her back the whole time, mostly praying for her to be healed. I had practiced Luke 18:1 faithfully for three years. I wasn't about to stop. I prayed and prayed and prayed with hope of seeing the miracle continue. I left Jan. 7 for Texas but planned to come back soon. As days passed, mom declined and my brother informed me that she was getting worse. He asked me to return sooner than planned. I immediately got on a plane with no plan for leaving her again.

Seeing my mom for the first time after a week was hard. She had clearly declined. I could hear it in her voice. My mom usually had a powerful voice, but it was weak and raspy. It was obvious she wasn't improving. I continued to pray believing God wasn't finished with her.

I think the thought of losing someone so close is very hard. Maybe I was praying more for me than for her as I didn't want to experience the pain from loss. As the days passed, mom didn't improve. Later, mother approached me to ask me to begin praying for God to take her to Heaven. Having ministry experiences with people close to death, I knew this wasn't a good sign for me. One thing I noticed when Jesus prepares to take people home is that the person about ready to go often asks people to pray they be taken to Heaven. It was hard to honor her request. No son who dearly loves his mother ever wants to pray such a prayer. So I didn't. I told mom that I was continuing in faith that God wasn't finished and that he'd bring healing to her body.

I believe I was more praying for myself than for her. Love is our greatest need, and one of the deepest bonds is between and mother and son. There are many people without a good bond with their mom. Many acknowledge the poor bond that leaves a hole in their heart. Many have this "soul hole" filled by the love of Jesus Christ. Only love can fill such a hole, but no matter how deep the love we have from or for people, only God truly fills the hole. Even though the experience with mom was traumatic and devastating, the deep hurt was a sign that no such "soul hole" was unfilled in me. Mom had invested her love in me.

BONDING WITH HER 'THIRD' CHILD

My wife flew out to be with me. As a full-time youth minister, her church graciously allowed her the time she needed to minister to her mother-in-law and I. Mom never told me or my younger brother that she desired a daughter—I never felt less for being a son—but there was something in me that knew mom wanted a daughter. One of the blessings from the hard time was how my wife cared for my mom. From nail clippings to foot massages, I know my mom bonded with her daughter-in-law during that time. I saw the caring side of my wife that excelled under these types of circumstances. Just four years earlier, her father passed away from esophageal cancer. She was there to care and serve her father. Now, God called on her again to serve a new but similar role. It was a daily, constant type of service where I saw the deep depths of character in my wife. Though grim and dire circumstances, God used this to show an aspect of my wife's character that otherwise I likely might not have seen. Jodi grew on mother a lot. Mom began thanking God for her three kids and one of the kids she was thankful for was her daughter-in-law.

Mom experienced the love of a daughter she'd never had but always wanted. The last time I saw my mom smile was when Jodi did her daily foot massage. It would always relax my mom and put her in a happy state. Jodi spent a long time massaging her mother-in-law's feet, and her mother-in-law greatly appreciated it.

LAST DAY

As the days passed, mom's condition continually declined. It seemed that God was preparing to take her home. February 15, 2009 arrived and mom asked for prayers for Heaven. Every night we prayed with mom she seemed more and more focused on Heaven and asking God to take her. I prayed the prayer for God to take her soon if it wasn't in his will to heal her. I had years and years of memories with mom since her diagnosis, more than three to be exact, and nightly prayer time was the most cherished time I had with her. I'm so glad for the many times of prayer with her. They are, and forever will be, in my heart.

The night of February 15, 2009 was the last time we prayed with mom. Mom, Jodi, and I gathered in her room. My heart desired more times of prayer, but one thing this world teaches is that tomorrow isn't guaranteed. We know to make the most of today. The last time I interacted with mom would be around 2 am. She often needed to go to the rest room at night, and I often helped her. She often told me she had a great son and that she loved him. I will always remember the last days. Around 2 am, I helped mom into the bathroom then back into bed. Had I known it would be the last time we interacted I would've done more.

MOM IS WITH JESUS

The next morning I woke up and noticed mom still sleeping. During her last days, I slept in the same room with her. I moved a bed right beside hers, and I was with her all the time in case she needed help. She often awoke early in the morning as sleeping was difficult for her. It was rare for her to sleep through the night, and she often awoke before 7 am. But this day, 7 am passed. She was still sleeping. 8 am passed, still sleeping. At first I was happy to see her rest so much. Her lack of sleep was a concern for me. As so much time passed I began to worry, finally around 10:20 am, we noticed mom's shirt was moist. I tried to wake her, mom's head went limp and she stopped breathing. The last thing mom would've heard in this world was my voice trying to wake her. I prayed to God asking him to bring her back, but there was peace in my heart that being with Jesus was a good thing. Later we gathered around her to pray, thanking God for her and for him allowing her into the Kingdom.

I'll never forget the day mom went to heaven. It was the loneliest and saddest day of my life. Tears uncontrollably streamed down my face. My heart felt emptiness and loss like never before. Though mom's passing ended one long journey for me, a new one was about to begin, a dark one into the world of grief.

ENDNOTES

1. Her sharing is on Youtube. Go to Youtube and type in Jane Chung and you can view her sharing.
2. Isaiah 55.

17

Grief

Tears are a tribute to our deceased friends. When the body is sown, it must be watered. But we must not sorrow as those that have no hope; for we have a good hope through grace both concerning them and concerning ourselves.
—Matthew Henry

Blessed are those who mourn, for they shall be comforted.
—Matthew 5:4

Grief is a gruff companion, like a thorn stuck in the heart. Nothing is more desirous than its quick removal, but it lodges deeper and longer than wanted.

Mother went home. As a believer in Christ, I should be happy for her. She was healed, no more suffering and pain because she was in the arms of Jesus. But within seconds of waking up in the mornings, tears flowed. It didn't seem real. My whole life, even before I was born, was connected to my mom. Now she was gone and grief replaced her companionship. How would I deal with it? Would I let her loss consume me? Would I never recover? Or would I accept the fact that life *is* loss and recover? Mom wouldn't want me to languish is sorrow and despair, so I needed to handle her homecoming in a way that would allow me to eventually move on. But I first needed to grieve.

Grief

Handling grief is important. The emotional situation is too enormous to ignore. Dealing with grief is one of the darkest most burdensome things I've faced. It's an awful feeling in the soul that can't immediately be removed. In some ways, a form of grief always remains quietly lurking in the shadows of my heart.

A friend shared something Jewish people do to deal with grief; they take seven days and focus on the lost loved one. Rather than entering back into work or life, the loss of the loved one becomes their life. Rather than focusing on activities that help them to keep their minds off the loved one or the sense of loss, their minds move toward the loved one. Intentional reflection and remembrance are invested with silence and solitude. It proved very wise and helpful advice and helped me reengage with the world by first allowing myself a period of grieving. It wouldn't be the only period. Jewish people take up to a year for their grief, but the first step was very helpful to me, also very painful.

I ceased working on my research for a week and spent a lot of time alone in mom's room.[1] It was odd and quiet. She was on oxygen the last two months of life, and although the machine was not too loud, the consistent, subtle hum could certainly be heard. The oxygen machine no longer ran, and the house was *so* quiet. The silence seemed louder than the machine ever was. It was surreal sitting in the silence of mom's room, empty and lifeless. Tears streamed from my eyes, enough to fill a small pond.

The focus of the week was to remember. Mom didn't like Italian food, but there was one restaurant she enjoyed. For dinner, I took Jodi there. My wife wondered if it was a good idea, but I knew I needed to do things like this. Tears flowed during dinner as I talked about times I'd eaten there with her and the many memories that came to mind as I thought of her. I ordered things she liked to order and ate dishes I knew she liked. It was hard, but God used these types of actions to heal.

Taking seven days of focused grief helped me reengage in life once the time ended. Grief is a horrible experience in some ways. Sleep is difficult. Eating is odd. The heart is sick and sad. A person's memory is shot; it's hard to live.

I spent a lot of time alone in my mom's room during the seven days. The deafening sound of silence constantly reminded me she was gone. Her hospital bed departed. Her nightstand vanished. Her medical chair moved out, and the room was left empty and lifeless without those tangible, painful reminders. It was good for me to engage my grief rather than try to deny it or go on as normal. Life wasn't the old normal; I needed to adjust to a new normal. After seven days, the pain was still there. My heart still hurt, but there was clearly a step taken in the healing process.

The Bible acknowledges that grief is a season of life that requires time.[2] At seven days the grief didn't suddenly end. In Genesis 50:3 the Bible talks about a seventy day mourning period. Forty days of embalming together with another thirty days. A friend explained to me that for a year, except on the Sabbath, Jewish people wear a black band around their arm. At the end of the year they take the band off as a symbol of ending their grief and re-entering life. In Deuteronomy 34:8, the nation of Israel observed thirty days of weeping and mourning, then Scripture says the period "came to an end". It's wise to accept a period of mourning before re-entering life. It can be a year, like the Jewish people, or longer. There's no one-size-fits-all time period. Although everyone mourns differently, the principle applied is that we accept that a time period exists where grief will be a gruff companion in our heart and mind. Its not usually a welcome guest, but it reminds us there's love. Grief inhabits a heart when some element of love or hope existed between people.

MOM GOT HER DAUGHTER; HER SON GOT A COMFORTER

One blessing was to see mom bond with her daughter-in-law. Jodi did a great job taking care of her mother-in-law, which made her last days more bearable. For over three years, mom's healing was my primary prayer, but I realized that if mom had been healed with 20 or more years of health, she may never have bonded with Jodi like she did the last month of her life. Jodi was finished caring for her mother-in-law now and had to focus on caring for her husband. I really needed it. Losing my mother at almost 39 years of age was a large loss. Much like God gave Rebecca to comfort Isaac, so he shared Jodi with me, knowing it would be much harder to go through the loss without her.[3]

SAN DIEGO

Mother requested to be cremated.[4] Eight days after her passing my brother called and told me the crematory finished the job and I was to retrieve mom's remains. Had I not engaged in those seven days of embracing grief, I could not have gone to that crematorium.

Family gathered together and flew to San Diego. Mom requested that her ashes be poured in the area where my father passed away 30 years ago. We fulfilled her wish. My brother's wife found a group that handles funerals at sea and made the arrangements. One of the greatest things a person can do for those enduring emotional strain is help them care for the sometime often tedious details in organizing the people and memorial event. In this case, my brother's wife handled locating a group coordinating funerals at sea that suited our purposes. It helped immensely.

We all arrived in San Diego and set sail for the La Jolla Beach area. Once we arrived, we threw flowers into the water, poured her ashes over the sea, and remembered she was gone but in a better place where we'll see her again.

It wasn't an easy time but it was good to be with family and friends. My uncle and his wife were very close to my mom. Being together gave us strength to move on. There's something satisfying about carrying out the wishes of those passed. Even though mother was gone, there was a sense that she was present that day. Her earthly remains were poured into the sea, but her soul lives forever to someday reunite with her body.

ENDNOTES

1. See also Genesis 50:10.
2. Genesis 38:12; Genesis 50:3–4; Deuteronomy 34:8; Psalm 31:9–24; Psalm 88:9–89:52;
3. Genesis 24:67
4. On the issue of Christianity and creamation, see Richard Mouw's blog at: http://www.netbloghost.com/mouw/?p=85

18

Why?

We do not choose the day of our birth nor may we choose the day of our death, yet choice is the sovereign faculty of the mind. When God loves a creature he wants the creature to know the highest happiness and the deepest misery He wants him to know all that being alive can bring. That is his best gift. There is no happiness save in understanding the whole.

—Thornton Wilder

For now we see in a mirror dimly, but then face to face; now I know in part, but then I will know fully just as I also have been fully known.

—1 Corinthians 13:12

THE PAIN I WAS feeling was deeper than anything I'd ever felt. Never had I felt so alone, never had I felt so lost, never had I felt so gloomy. Mom was healed in heaven and prayers for healing ceased. I'd faithfully and continuously prayed for over three years, applying Scripture, believing God's greatness, and even having signs that the prayers would be answered here on earth, but mother was gone and darkness crept in.

I still remember the first Sunday service I attended after mom's homecoming. She died on a Monday, so I had almost a week. Singing songs about God brought doubt for the first time in my life. I questioned

God's goodness, kindness and even his existence. The suffering and hurt lead me face-to-face with the question: do I really believe in God?

Loss leads people to face who they believe God is. Rabbi Harold Kushner's book *When Bad Things Happen to Good People* was his response to the pain of losing his teenage son to a rare disease. Kushner concluded that evil exists in this world because God is powerless to stop it. Now, I had to come up with my own answers to the same questions: Why? Who is God to me? Do I accept Kushner's answer that God wasn't powerful enough to help my mom or do I continue believing that his ways are higher but trustworthy?

In the midst of affliction, many ask *why*? Job asked God why? My mom asked God why? Now I was the one doing the asking. Closely related to the issue was: who is God? Do I really know God? Who is the focus on? Was the focus of my life myself and forwarding my agenda or was I truly focused on God and had him as my priority? Mom was gone, but I was still here. She no longer had to ask questions, but I did. The answers would determine the course for the rest of my life.

I really would never know why. When Job asked why, God never told him. Even though the adversary challenged God and bet that Job would fall away from him, God never told Job about his wager or that he had passed. God only told Job about himself. He asked Job where he was when the world was being created and appealed to his creation. Job didn't leave God with any answers but he left with something better: God.

This leads to the second question: who is God? If I was honest, my answer would've been that God is a "Cosmic Santa Clause." He exists for me. I give him my list and he's responsible to execute it. My attitude was often, "this is my will God, bless it," instead of the more biblical "thy will be done." If this is all God is to me, he's not very big; but I am.

Pain often robs rationality. When experiencing deep suffering, often, the first instinct is relief. Relief is rooted in circumstances. In order for relief to be real circumstances need to change. God taught Job that relief isn't circumstantial but theological and personal, union with God through knowing and believing in him brings relief.

Pain often reveals our real image of who God is to us. A professor once told me that after the Holocaust during World War II, half of the Jewish survivors left their faith while the other half drew closer. I was face-to-face with the same decision: do I leave God or do I stay? If I stay, my view of God can't remain the same; if I leave, it means I no longer want to know God for who he is. God gave Job one answer, himself. Job responded in worship; now it was my turn.

God first revealed to Job that he was creator of the cosmos, one can see his greatness in the sky. Job 38: 6–7, 31 "On what were its bases sunk, or who laid its cornerstone, when the morning stars sang together and all the sons of God shouted for joy? . . . Can you bind the chains of the Pleiades or loose the cords of Orion?"

Pondering astronomy leads one to God. When I meditate and reflect on how vast our universe is, I feel really small and God seems larger than anything I can imagine. The nearest solar system to ours is Andromeda, which is about two million light years away. How far is that? The speed of light is 3 times ten to the eight meters per second. If I stood on the equator of the earth a shot a bullet at the speed of light, it would go through me seven times in one second. If I took the same gun and shot it at Andromeda, it would take two million years to reach it. Yet our galaxy, the Milky Way, and Andromeda are two of 100 billion galaxies in our universe. No wonder God appealed to the celestial when answering Job. When the facts about our universe are evident, humankind is very small while God is enormously big. It's a very humbling thought.

God wasn't done and appealed to the created world, specifically the animal kingdom. Job 39:1–3, "Do you know when the mountain goats give birth? Do you observe the calving of the does? Can you number the months that they fulfill, and do you know the time when they give birth, when they crouch, bring forth their offspring, and are delivered of their young?" Philip Yancey writes:

> A nearly invisible ice fish swims among the icebergs of Arctic and Antarctic waters, its survival made possible by the unique properties of its blood. A special protein acts as an antifreeze to keep ice crystals from forming, and its blood has no hemoglobin, or red pigment. As a result, the fish is virtually transparent.
>
> The instinctive navigational ability of common ducks, geese, and swans makes them the envy of the aircraft industry. On their trips south, some of the geese maintain a speed of fifty miles per hour, and fly 1,000 miles before making their first rest stop.
>
> When it comes to navigation, polar bears are no slouches either. A polar bear that is tranquilized, trapped, and released 300 miles away can usually find its way home, even across drift ice that changes constantly and holds no landmarks and few odors. But bears and birds are rank amateurs compared to lowly salmon, who

cruise the expanse of the Pacific Ocean for several years before returning (by scent? magnetic field?) to the streams of their birth.[1]

Indeed, God's creation reveals an aspect of himself that helps us understand his grandeur and our finitude.[2]

Next to the Bible, Tony Dungy's thoughts encouraged and comforted me the most.[3] Three days before I heard for the first time that my mother was ill, coach Dungy lost his son.[4] Just like myself, Rabbi Kushenr and scores of others, Dungy had to face who God was for himself. In an article from ESPN.com by Michael Smith, Dungy shares from the heart of how he reconciles the death of his son with his faith in God: "The Lord has a plan, We always think the plans are A, B, C and D, and everything is going to be perfect for us and it may not be that way, but it's still his plan. A lot of tremendous things are going to happen, it just may not be the way you see them . . . I've said all along that God is in control, . . . I have to believe that he's in control here, too." Like Dungy, I had to decide who God was. I chose to follow Dungy's view instead of Kushner's: God is in control and can be trusted and loved. I'll continue to follow Him.

Psychologists would rate that losing a child is more emotionally taxing than losing a parent. Dungy faced his greatest loss, a loss tough to recover from yet the pain didn't drive him away from God but toward him. Dungy didn't confuse God with life and continued believing in his faith despite losing his son. It was his words and example that helped me deal with the loss of my mom.

Despite having a walking example of loss, the pain didn't leave. I needed time to mourn, time to grieve, these would prove to be the only reliable antidotes. Weeks and months of tears was the path I needed to take in order to heal.

ENDNOTES

1. Philip Yancey, *Finding God in Unexpected Places* (Ann Arbor, MI: Servant Publications, 1997), 27–28.
2. Romans 1:20–21.
3. Tony Dungy is formally a head coach in the NFL, most notably, the Indianapolis Colts.
4. http://sports.espn.go.com/nfl/feature/featureVideo?page=amazinggrace

19

See You in Heaven

Other men see only a hopeless end, but the Christian rejoices in an endless hope.
—Gilbert M. Beeken

And I saw the holy city, new Jerusalem, coming down out of heaven from God, made ready as a bride adorned for her husband . . . [4] and He will wipe away every tear from their eyes; and there will no longer be *any* death; there will no longer be *any* mourning, or crying, or pain; the first things have passed away."
—Revelation 21:2, 4

Time heals as it passes. Although I still have days where missing mom produces tears, my heart is healthier.

Beyond hurt and pain, healing takes place and the heart grows, possessing a greater capacity to accept the things of the world that come and be less enamored with things here on earth. There will always be a soft and special place in my heart for mom, so I recognize that from time to time tears will likely come. But the tears have become friends that remind me of a kind of love that remains in a heart forever.

As I reflect on the years with my mom some thoughts come to mind. Despite being the most tumultuous time of my life so far, I see that my heart and soul have a greater capacity to spiritually grow. God bent my heart and soul in order to heal them. Just as muscle tissue gets strained and stretched in order to be strengthened and built up, the heart and soul experiences strain and stretching to be shaped anew. Trials and suffering offer some of the best opportunity for this to occur. The lactic acid of pride, arrogance, and insecurity get battered and beaten by suffering.

Another reflection is the currency of time with loved ones. We mistake dollars, yen, loonies, gold and silver as important currencies. These have their place, but once the basic necessities of food, shelter, bills, leisure, and clothing are taken care of, money's usefulness doesn't produce as much utility as we think. Time with loved ones, in my opinion, is our greatest currency. The old saying "money can't buy happiness" is true. Time with those we value and love does bring happiness. Assess the important people in our lives—parents, family, close friends—and order our priorities around time with them.[1] Time with God and people makes us the richest.

Another thing learned was the necessity of community. A person can't thrive in the Christian life without companions who share the same desire to walk faithfully with God. Though history records people like the Desert Fathers and Mothers who escaped wicked and dangerous Rome for solitude with the Lord, I argue that their example isn't modeled in Holy Scripture and shouldn't be looked upon as an ideal goal. For me, I needed community to continue the journey and am convinced that the prayers of the saints made a deep impact on me as well as my mom.

Life is hard. We all experience ups and downs in life. Sometimes life is really good, but other times it's bitter and painful. Despite how tough life can be, God reigns.[2]

Prayer with mom was so sweet. I've said it so many times before: I wish I'd done it more before mom was ever sick. I still hear her sweet voice praying child-like prayers to God. Though these thoughts sometimes bring tears, the tears are friendly reminders of the deep love that still lives in my heart. Love encounters pain, but pain reminds us that experiencing love makes the pain worth it.

I now wait for *my* time to go to heaven. I realize more and more that this world is temporary and passing away. Heaven is a place of perfection and joy where we reunite with loved ones and see the Savior face-to-face. The long journey in this world ends and life in Heaven begins. Eternity is reality, and Heaven is my true home. This earth is just a place I pass through.

Praying with Mom

Philip Yancey writes about future hope fueling present reality. During World War II, Americans in a German prison camp built a homemade radio. Americans received the news on the radio that Germany had surrendered. This news changed the whole countenance of the camp. Yancey writes:

> For three days the prisoners were hardly recognizable. They sang, waved at guards, laughed at the German shepherd dogs, and shared jokes over meals. On the fourth day, they awoke to find that all Germans had fled, leaving the gates unlocked. The time of waiting had come to an end.
>
> Here is the question I ask myself: As we Christians face contemporary crises, why do we respond with such fear and anxiety? Why don't we, like the Allied prisoners, act on the good news we say we believe? What is faith, after all, but believing in advance what will only make sense in reverse?[3]

This is the hope that I have to fight despair, loneliness, insecurity, hurt and pain. I know a better world is coming and need to live it! I know God makes all things new and never again allows death to sting me or the groans of this world to harm me. Loved ones who are in him will not be lost, we'll see them again, Christ has come and will come again.

I'm pretty sure that when I arrive at the gates of Heaven, mom will be there to greet me. I won't be surprised if she's the first one there to welcome me into glory. It will be a glorious day seeing her again. Though being reunited with her is strong motivation, the greater desire is to see my Savior and Lord. Praying with mom helped me experience the joy of walking closer and trusting my Savior more. It's he that I look forward to seeing together with my mom!

ENDNOTES

1. This does not take away the need to spend time with those who are not believers. One should have time with those needing the gospel also as a priority.
2. Romans 8:28.
3. Philip Yancey, *Grace Notes* (Grand Rapids: Zondervan, 2009), 221.

www.ingramcontent.com/pod-product-compliance
Lightning Source LLC
Chambersburg PA
CBHW050832160426
43192CB00010B/1999